AF593575

MANOEUVRE OF PLENTY

WORKS BY EDITH KOLLATH

DISTANZ

CONTENT / INHALT

TEXTS / TEXTE

WORKS / WERKE

ADDENDUM / ANHANG

it to be

it, then,

it, on

it would

it might.

it; and

it, till

it appears

it still

a short time, it

at last

»THE POETRY OF THE IMMATERIAL: EDITH KOLLATH'S AERIAL IMAGINATION«

BY CHRISTINA GRAMMATIKOPOULOU

Images of aerial imagination either evaporate or crystallize. We must seize them between the two poles of this constantly active ambivalence.

GASTON BACHELARD[1]

The meandering path of a gust of air: forming rings of smoke and clouds of vapour, caressing the folds of a fabric, sliding onto sheets of paper, filling bodies with the vital force of breath and leaving them to explore other bodies and environments.

It is a poem of open possibilities, energy and ephemerality, created by artist Edith Kollath.

Kollath incorporates the invisible and the immaterial as structural elements of her delicate objects and installations. Her creations come to life through subtle movements and sounds, breathing in space. This breath becomes perceived by the viewers as a gentle breeze, which introduces them into a meditative state.

Kollath has a wide fan of visual expression – from video to sculpture and installation, from abstract forms to concrete objects and human figures – always maintaining a minimalist elegance and a calm eloquence.

These are the kind of elements that shape ***BW1*** (2006); in this work, the video frame offers the view of a bathtub filled with water, almost still, apart from the slightly rippling surface. As the water drains out, it uncovers a female torso that moves as she breathes. The dramatic light pointing to the lower part of her body offers a revelation of the "origin of the world"; however, the structural and conceptual

1 Gaston Bachelard. *Air and Dreams, An Essay on the Imagination of Movement*, Dallas: The Dallas Institute, 1988 (1943), p.13.

centre of the composition is her gently oscillating navel, highlighting respiration as the most important act in the video.

Breath as a tool of harmony and a means of communication: this notion pervades the work ***in between*** (2007), a video showing a man and a woman exchanging breaths. Respiration is represented by a gust of smoke, that moves rhythmically from one mouth to another, bringing them both to a state of equilibrium and happiness, as their faces reveal. To feel someone's breath is a sign of intimacy, experienced only among people who are close to each other. However, to a certain extent, we all exchange air with each other and the environment, as Luce Irigaray observes: "[breathing] signifies a sharing with the world that surrounds me and with the community that inhabits it".[2]

As we move past the screen, into the space of an exhibition, the same gust of air reaches the audience. In the installation ***again, again*** (2009) a cloud of vapour becomes visible against a black background, before it disperses in the exhibition space, merging with the breaths of the visitors and becoming a collective visual and bodily experience. At the same time, the rings of vapour change formations and stimulate the imagination; it is a fragile, ephemeral construction that depends on chance and natural phenomena.

Chance becomes a decisive factor in ***nothing will ever be the same*** (2009). In this installation a translucent cloth is set in motion, getting lifted up in the air and then falling over and over again by means of an automatic mechanism. The repetitive, rhythmic action gives a different visual result every time. Therefore the cloth becomes a sculpture that changes and moves incessantly, taking random shapes by air and gravity. As the cloth falls and rises, the air sneaks into its folds, showing its invisible body -with an almost human-like corporeity. The cloth acquires a life of its own, like a dancer that leaps into the void, making a minimal impact against the hard surface of the floor. During the next fall the cloth will

2 Irigaray, Luce. "From The Forgetting of Air to To Be two", in: Nancy Holland and Patricia Huntington, *Feminist Interpretations of Martin Heidegger*, Pennsylvania 2001, S. 309.

'improvise' a new choreography, completing a different orbit through the air and landing in a different spot. Within this movement, "every breath of air is brought to life. It is a scrap of air's flesh that had at one time been alive, an aerial fabric that will clothe a soul".[3]

Smoother in motion and equally lyrical in tone, ***disport*** (2009) invites the viewers in a pentagonal cell made of textiles that sway inwards and outwards, as the lights change from bright to dimmer. In this installation, the artist delimits a space that is open to expansion and in constant exchange with its surroundings, like a human body that breathes and moves into the open. The artwork invites the viewers to connect to their corporeity, to reach a state of enhanced awareness of one's self and surroundings, where the perception of the artwork passes through the entire body, and not simply the eyes and the mind. The visual and the corporeal coexist in harmony.

These two elements, with the addition of logos (words), are present in ***thinking I'd last forever*** (2008). The artwork consists of antique editions of classical books, that are allowed to "breathe" through the installation of microprocessors in their interior; hence, apart from an individual appearance and content, each book is granted with its individual breathing rhythm, slowly raising its cover and opening the pages as if someone was browsing through them. At a time when printed books have begun to become obsolete, Edith Kollath manages to give a new life to old editions, by combining the classical format of the book with contemporary technology. These books, after having "absorbed" the breaths of the numerous readers that have browsed through them throughout their existence, now return those breaths to the visitors of the installation; with their gentle movement, they tempt a new generation of readers to discover the knowledge and imagination that is hidden within those pages, which is still relevant and open to discussion, despite the fact that it took its final form a long time ago.

---

3 Bachelard 1988, p.230.

Going from the final form to the initial idea, ***sigh*** (2011) seems to be making a tribute to the creative process which often involves papers thrown on the floor, taking random morphs by the hand that has discarded them. In the installation crumpled black papers become plasticised into permanent sculptures, elevated to the status of art. As their elegant shape is projected against the white exhibition space, the work becomes a collaborative action between a spontaneous gesture and a conscious preservation.

If it were a sheet of paper (2011) follows the same lines; a crumpled silk paper floats in space above a mirror surface, like a cloud reflecting itself on water. The defiance of the laws of physics stimulates a curiosity and playfulness in the viewers, who are challenged to see if they can blow it away. At the same time, this denial of gravity, the constant postponement of a pending fall, creates a field of energy between the paper and its reflection.

A conservation of energy, a state of inertia and a rhythmic motion: ***pendulum lucidum*** (2011) is a reconstruction of Newton's cradle with light bulbs, shaped by multiple forces. There are two different oscillations taking place in the pendulum, the gentle change from brightness to darkness, as the bulbs light up and down slowly, and the swaying of the bulbs, that needs to be set in motion by an exterior agent. Thus, the artwork becomes the meeting point between an interior rhythm and an interaction with the environment.

Similarly, ***trying to expand the potential of love I can give*** (2011) is built on this meeting point, where fleeting reflections, waves of light and an engulfing darkness interact. In this installation, a set of semi-transparent mirrors are propped on a piece of wood, sheltering a light bulb that stands behind them. As the light becomes dimmer and brighter, it creates multiple reflections between the mirrors; at the same time, the somehow diffracted reflection of the observer disappears or becomes clearer, as the intensity of light fades in and out. It is a reflection that dissolves to reveal what lays behind, just like visual a psychological depth that needs to be discovered behind a face. This way, the mirrors become the limit where the exhibition space blends with the infinite, and appearances disintegrate to reveal the invisible.

Edith Kollath appears to be creating forms that acquire a life of their own, growing into space; this is seen in ***ligeia*** (2010), a fragile construction of wire and ribbon, that appears to be floating into its surroundings like a water creature, and her Tape series ***untitled (tape)*** (2010-11), where the transparent tape lines seem to be dancing on the dark background, against some unfelt undercurrent that scatters them and puts them again in order. Her abstract ***lines and space*** (2009) drawings display the same desire to move, as they crawl and spread in the deep space of the black paper. In ***untitled (tape-text)*** (2011) the tape lines are put in order, one behind the other, to hold the words of a poem; the words of the poem seem to be breathed out randomly, yet through repetition and difference they are weaved into a visual and literary meaningful structure, that provides insight on the work of Kollath, as a connective thread that brings together gusts of air, changes of matter and oscillations of light and darkness.

The artist's consistency in using fine winding lines, transparencies and dark spaces creates a unity within the corpus of her work, despite the diversity of media that she employs.

Edith Kollath's "aerial imagination" creates ethereal visions that are rooted into immateriality and ephemerality and flow outwards to reach the viewers' bodies. Her work is meant to be lived with all the senses, becoming a transient but powerful experience. As the viewers enter a world of calm movements and repetitive sounds, rhythmic breaths and soft lights, they discover an unknown path towards intellectual nourishment, collective communication and interior balance.

Edith Kollath's art finds the way to extend beyond the walls of the exhibition space: it becomes a lasting experience, one that lingers in memory for a long time.

BARCELONA, FEBRUARY 2013

BW 1

Smilefaucet – AIR, Fontana's, New York 2007

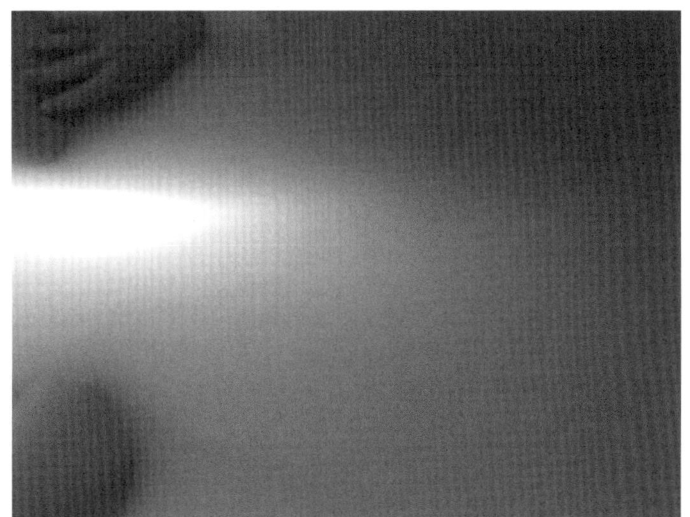

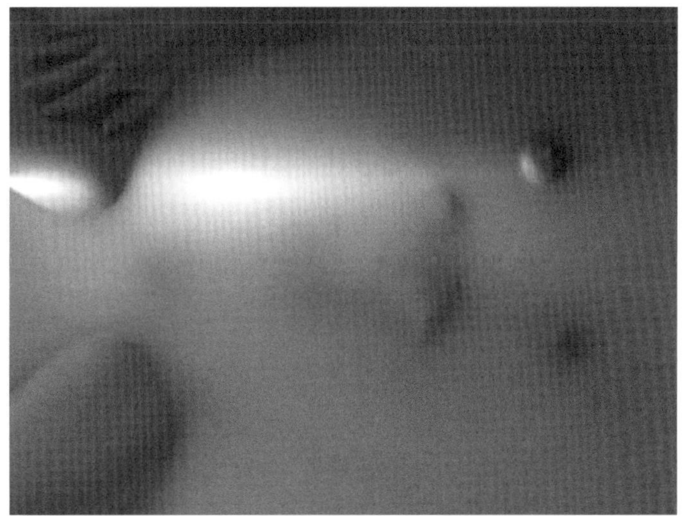

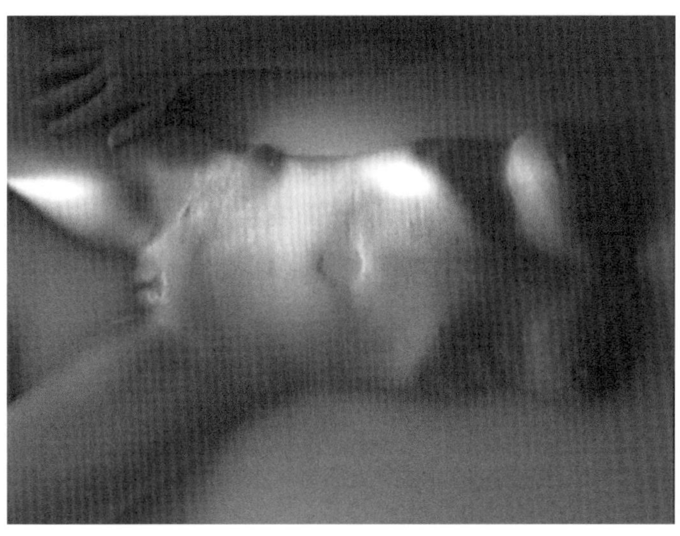

IN BETWEEN

Smilefaucet – AIR, Fontana's, New York 2007

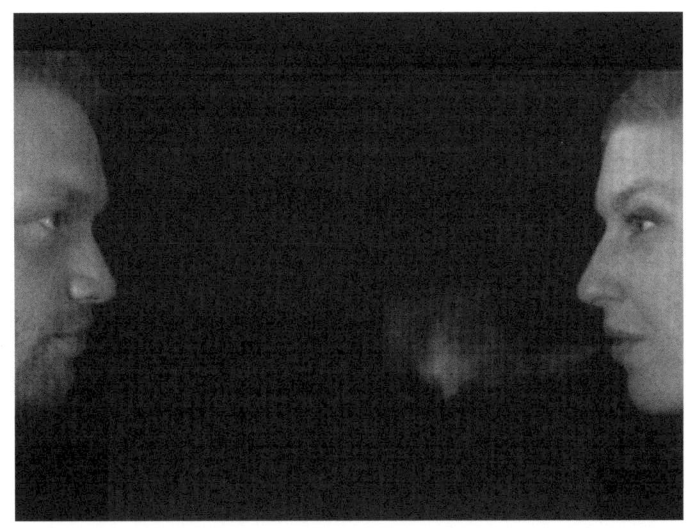

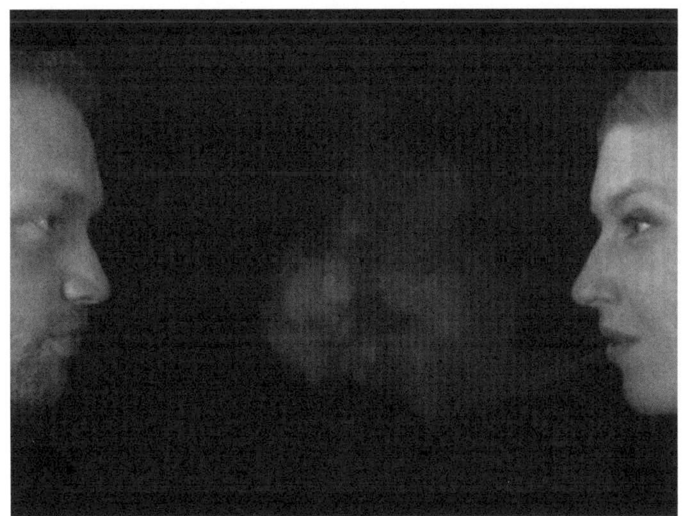

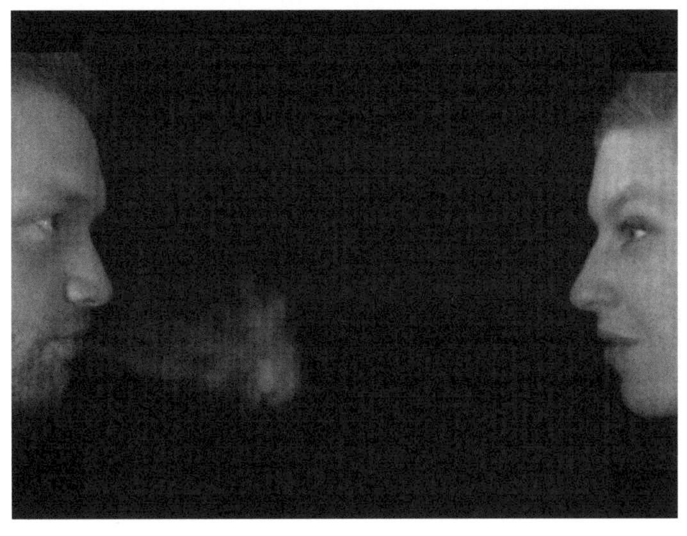

AGAIN, AGAIN

installation view,
COLLECTIVA gallery, Berlin 2009

emerged

began to vanish

once more.

to and fro,

upon for ever.

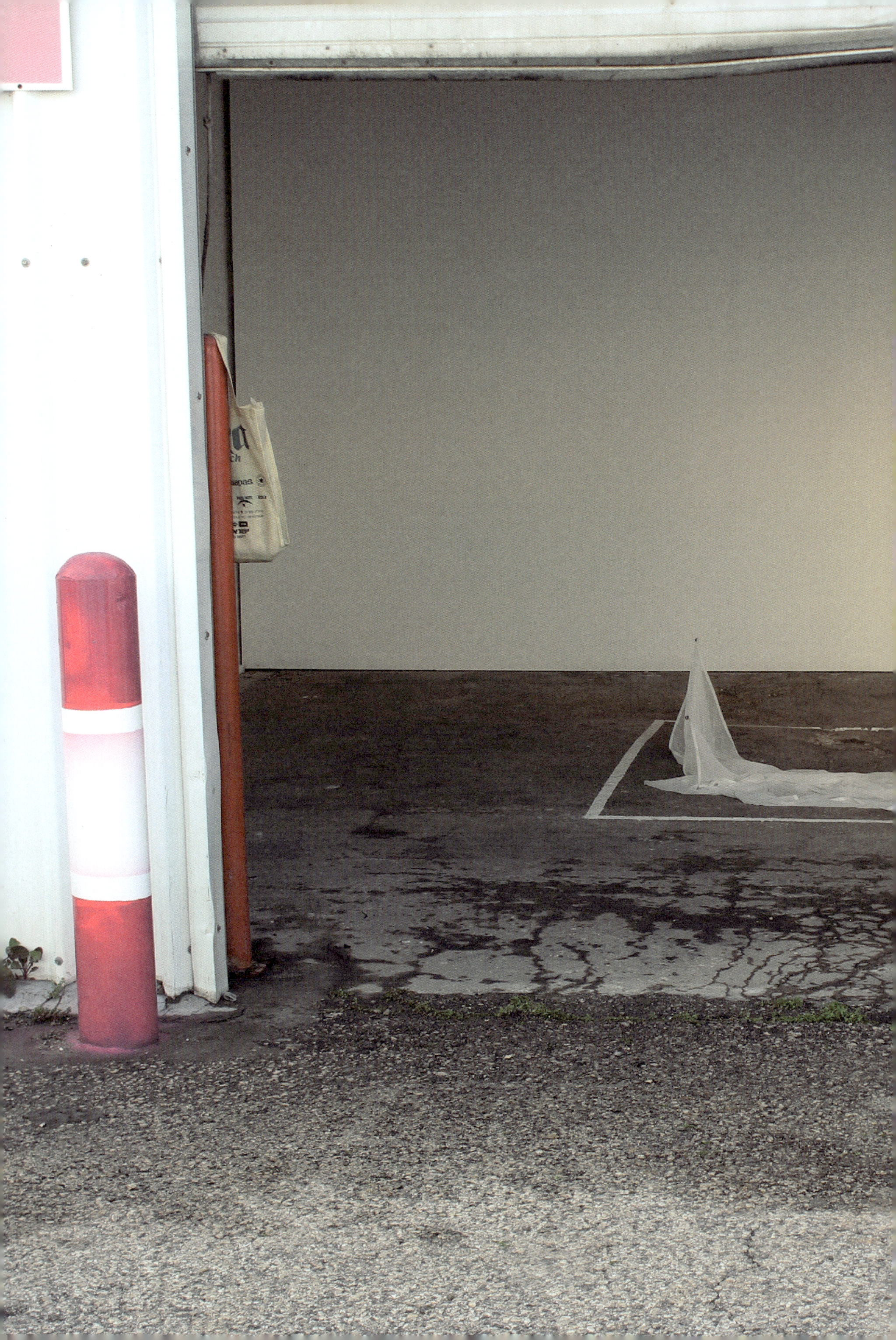

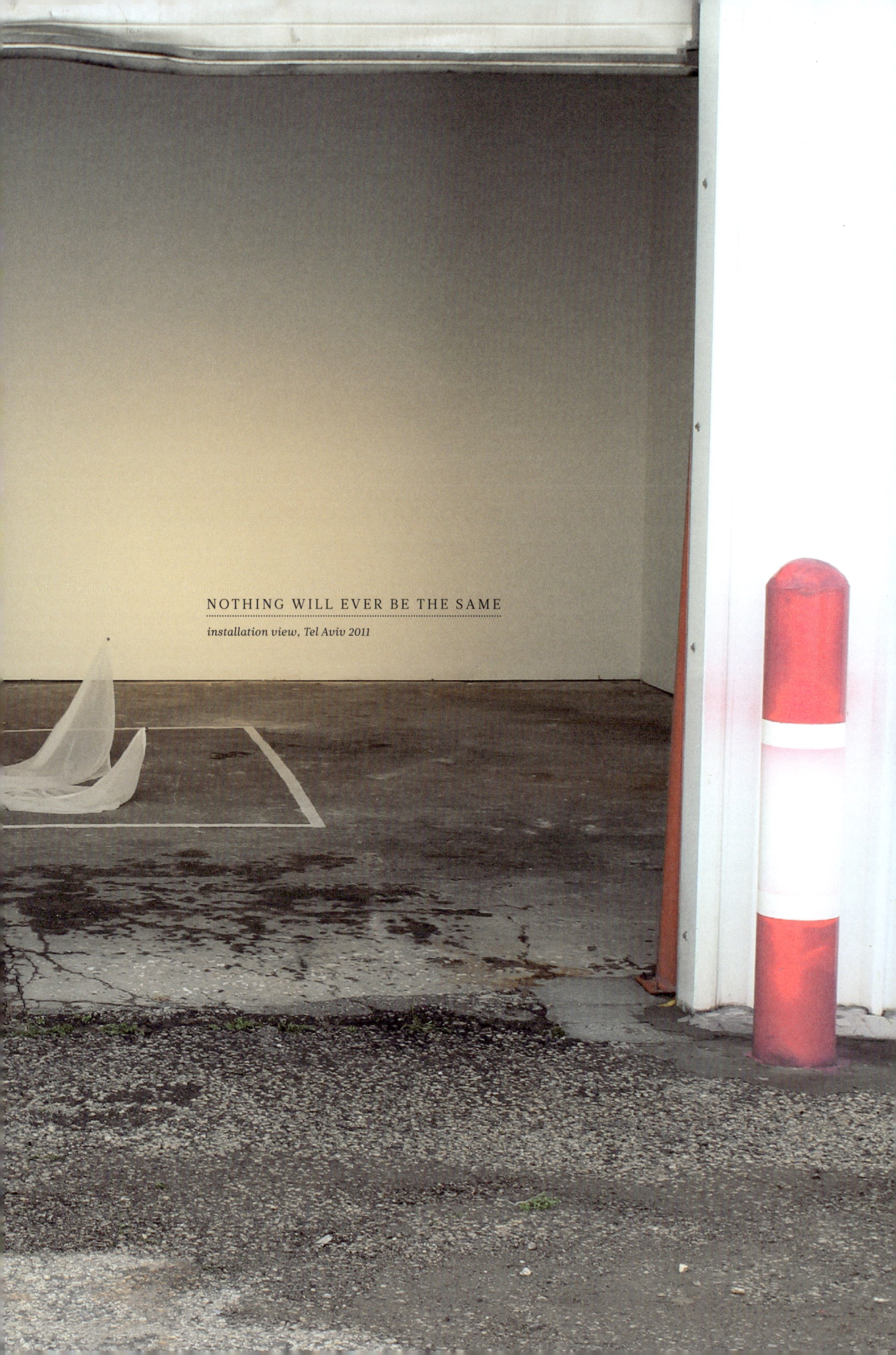

NOTHING WILL EVER BE THE SAME

installation view, Tel Aviv 2011

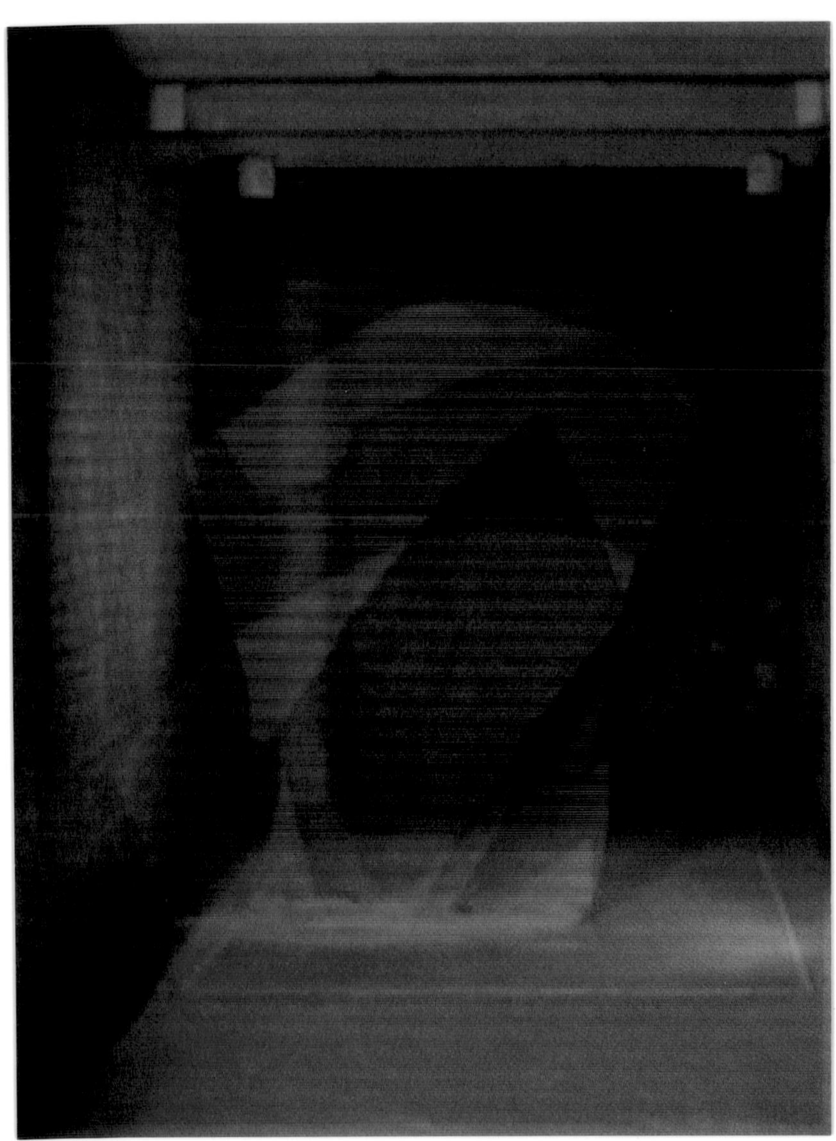

Ringen, installation view, CREAM Contemporary, Berlin 2009

Einatem,

↑ Inspiration

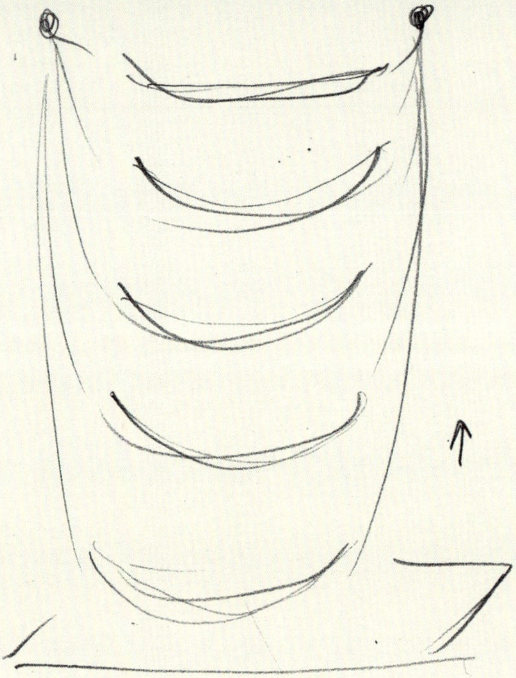

↑

Kraft schöpfen,

auf ein höheres Energieniveau anheben,
ähnliche Form, dehnen, weiten, ausbreiten

Martin: 646 - 351 - 2269

↓ Ausatem,

Expiration

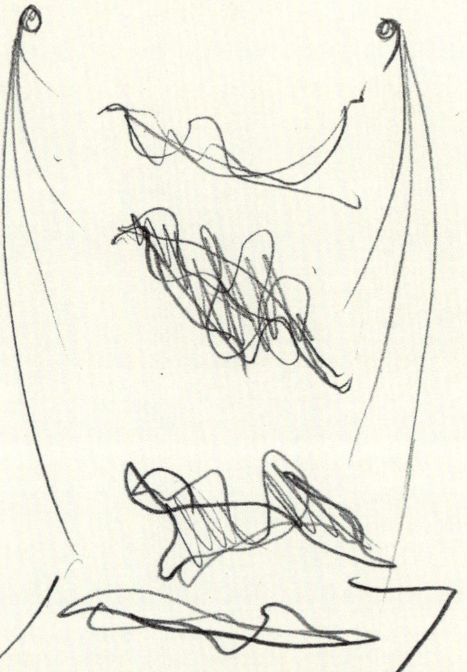

ewige Wiederholung,
niemals ist der Ausatem
das Fallen gleich
Differenz der Wiederholung

Fallen, Gestalten, sich ausdrücken,
Formen, schöpferische Phase, „Wolken gucken"

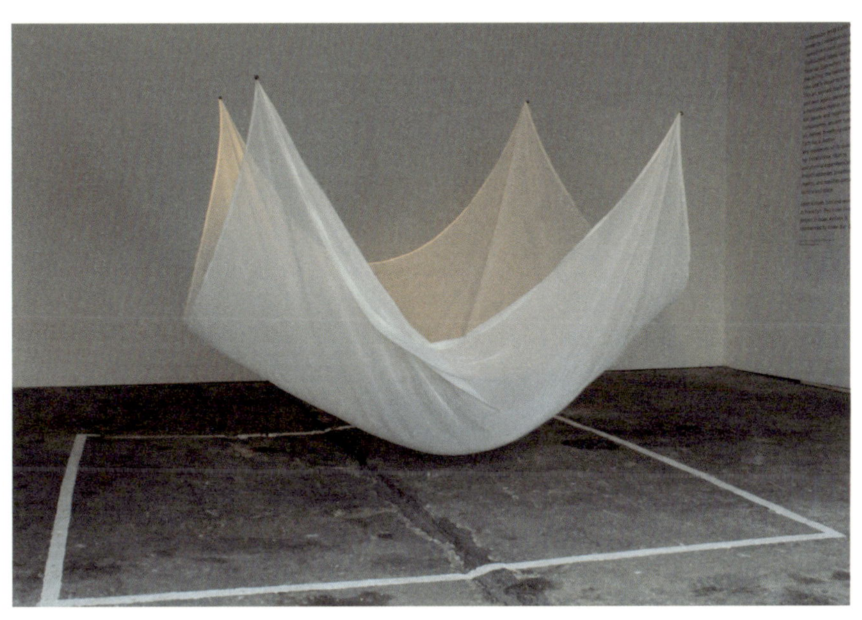

NOTHING WILL EVER BE THE SAME

special guests, installation view,
fresh paint contemporary art fair,
Tel Aviv 2011

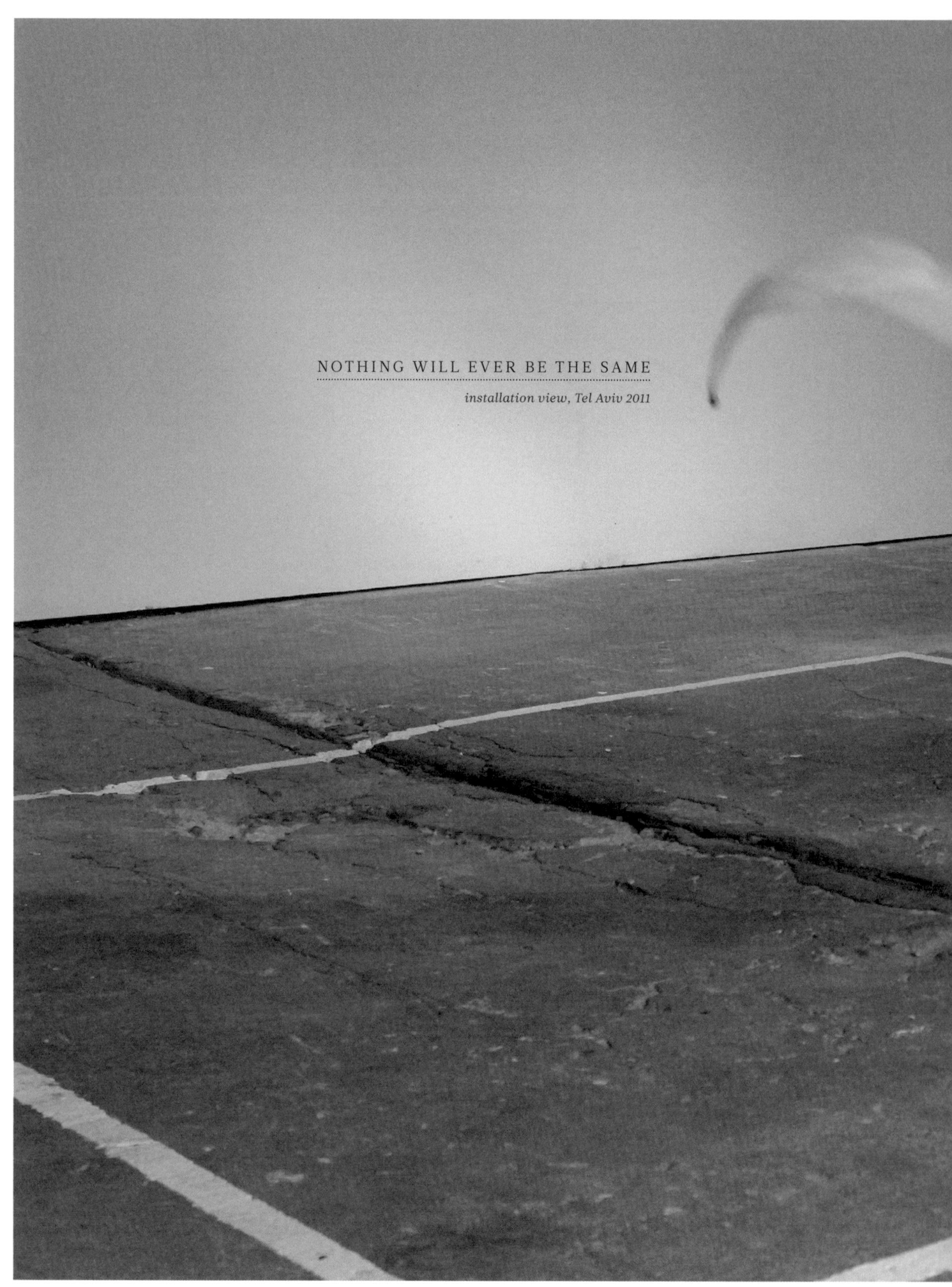

NOTHING WILL EVER BE THE SAME

installation view, Tel Aviv 2011

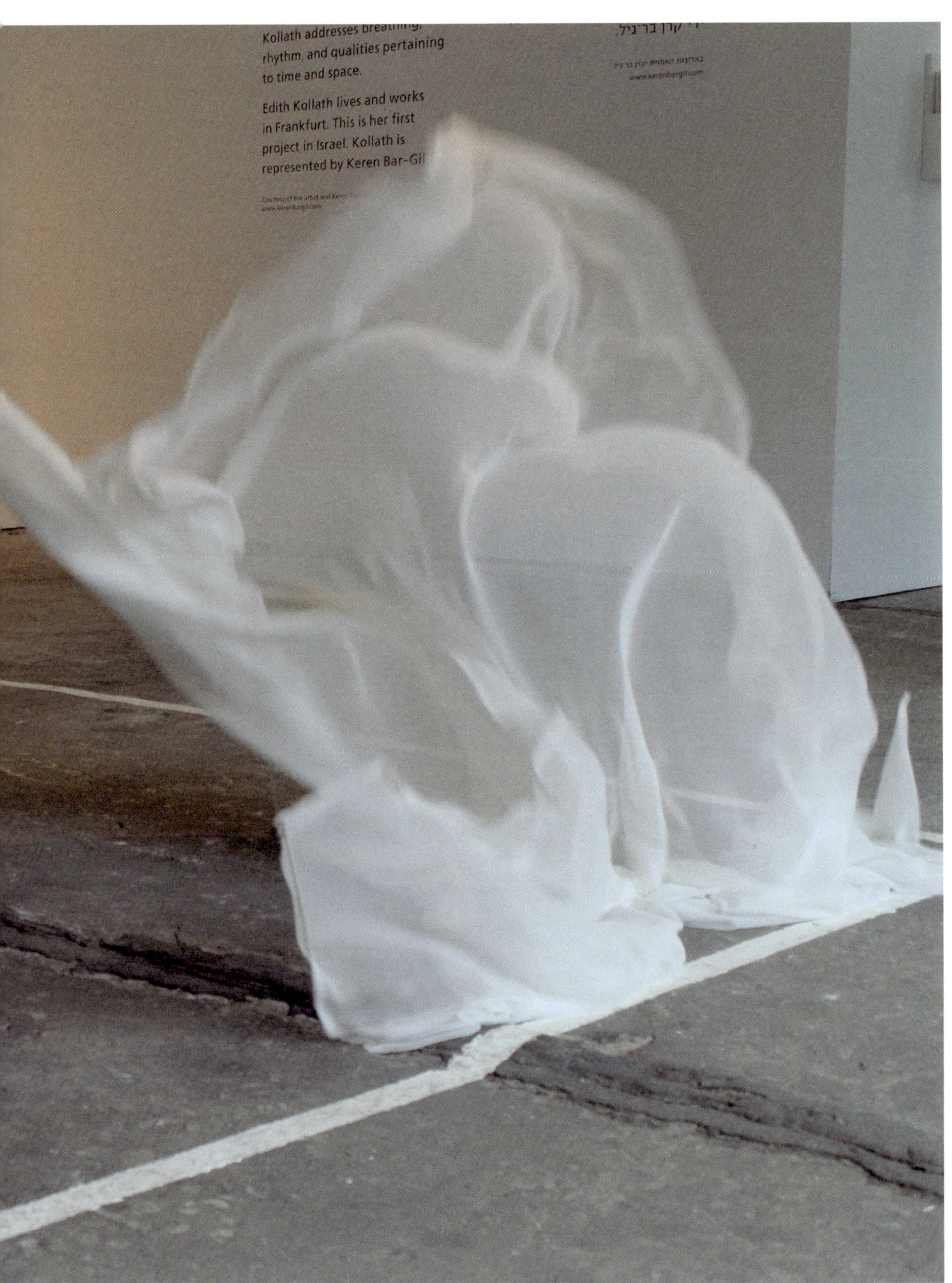
Kollath addresses breathing,
rhythm, and qualities pertaining
to time and space.
Edith Kollath lives and works
in Frankfurt. This is her first
project in Israel. Kollath is
represented by Keren Bar-Gi

for the future,

for the future

frame of things.

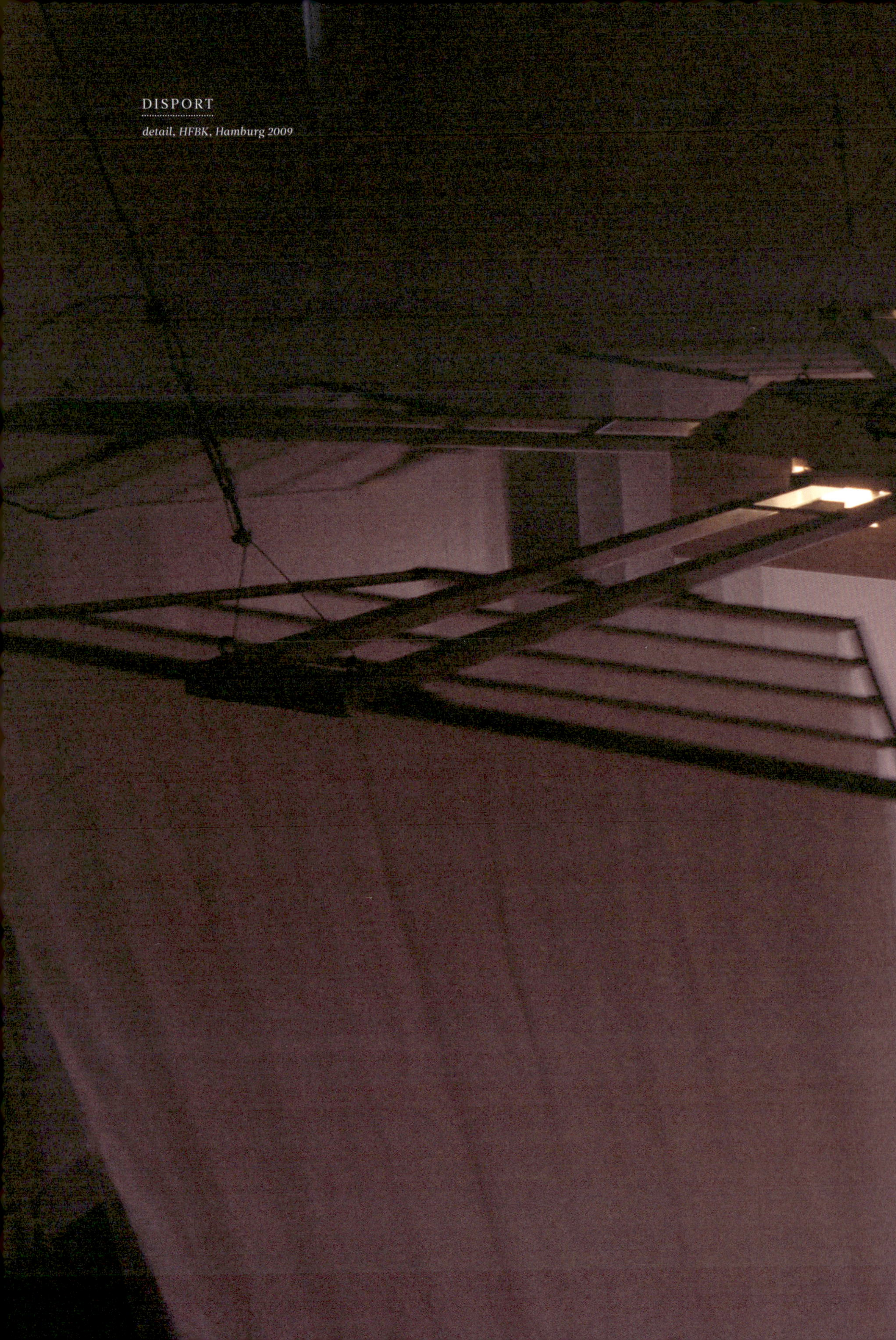

DISPORT

detail, HFBK, Hamburg 2009

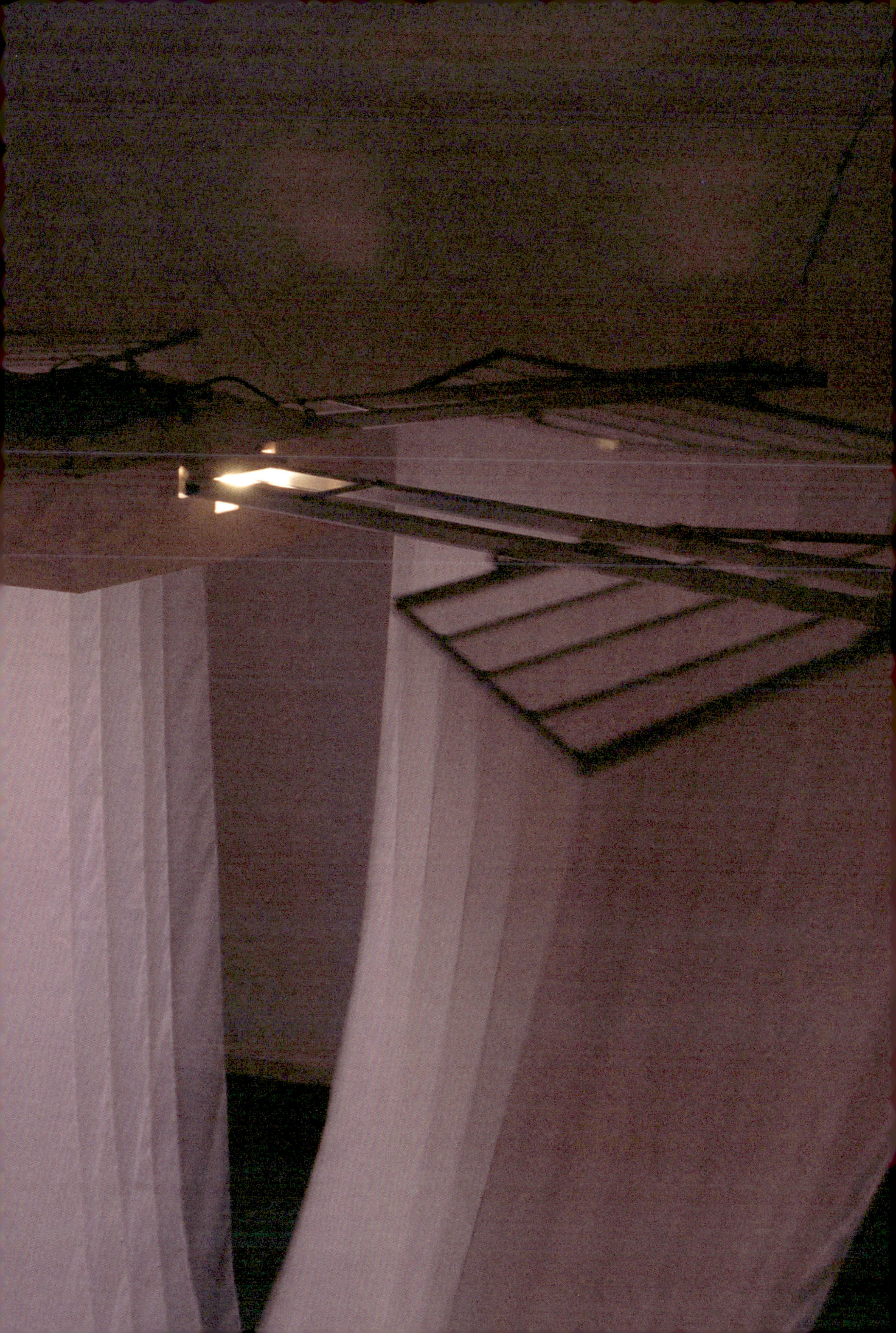

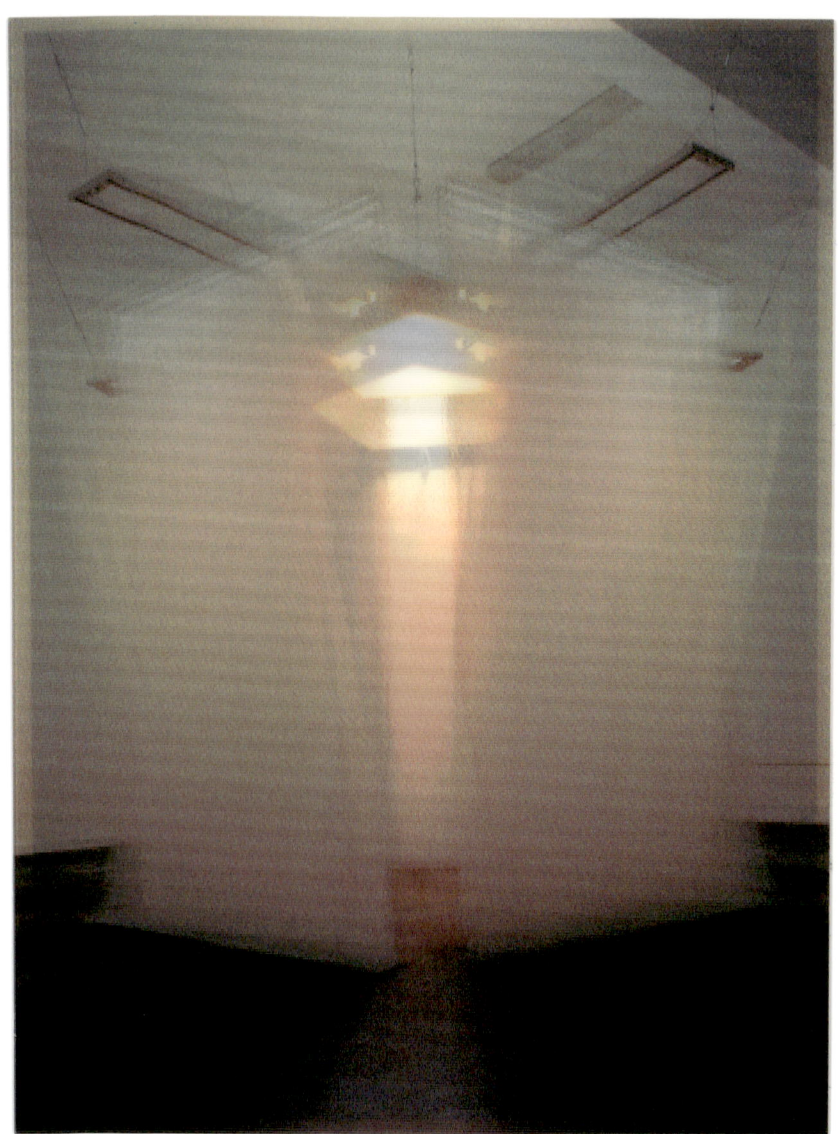

DISPORT

installation view, HFBK, Hamburg 2009

```
boolean finished=false;
while(!finished)        //solange noch nicht alle Endschalter erreicht sind...
{
  //if (speed/4>150)
  speed--;
  finished=true;
  for (int i=0; i<5; i++){
    if (!flags[i]) {
      //analogWrite(motorpins[i],speed/4);
      analogWrite(motorpins[i],min(255,max(150, speed)));

      //Endschalter testen, und "finished" setzen, wenn ALLE gedrueckt wurden.
      // der jeweilige Motor stoppt aber sofort.
      if(digitalRead(limitswitches[i])==1){
         analogWrite(motorpins[i],30);
         flags[i]=true;
      }
      finished=false;
    }
  }
  delay(10);

  //Licht einen Schritt ausblenden
  analogWrite(LIGHT,min(255,max(0,brightness--)));

}
```

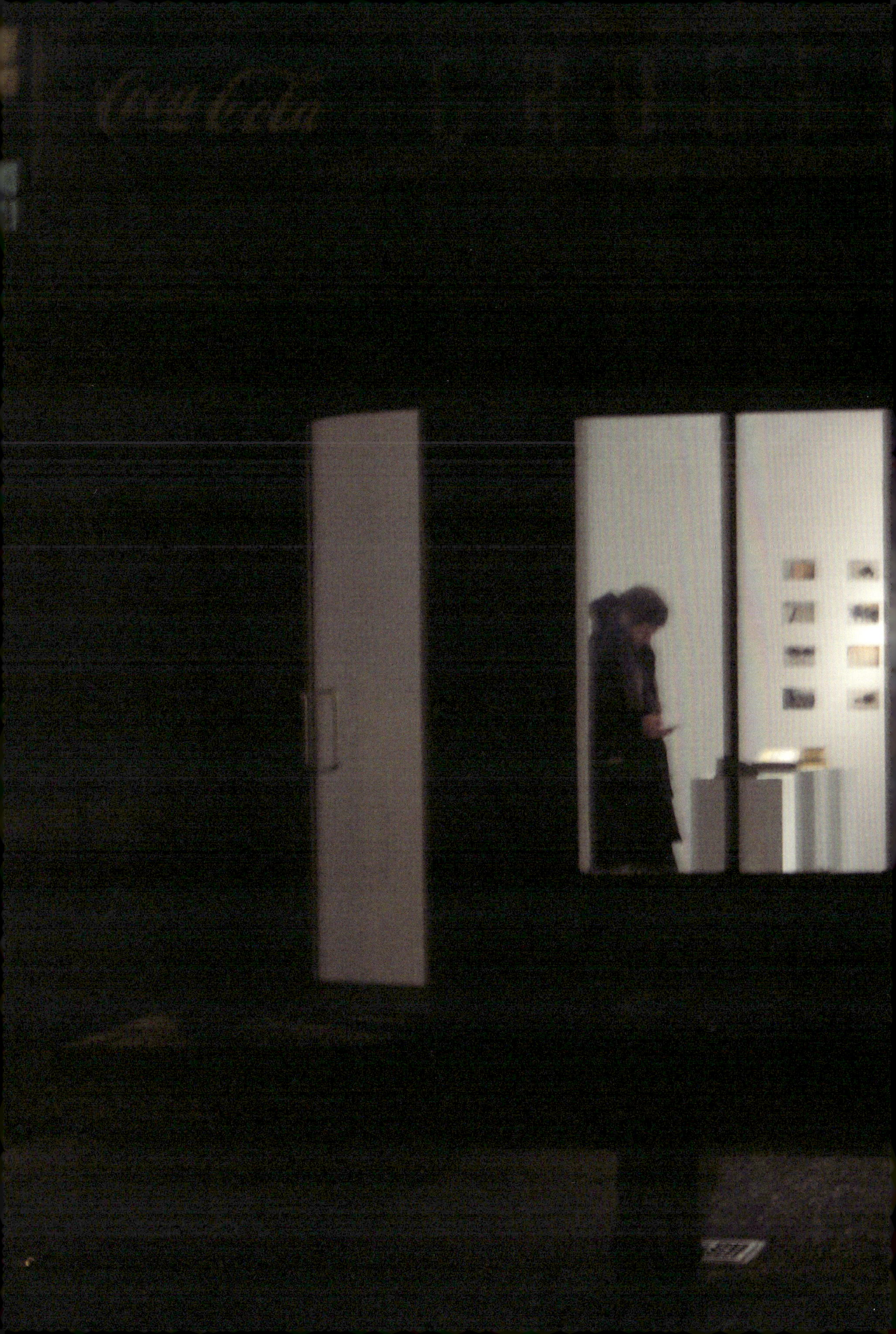
Coca-Cola

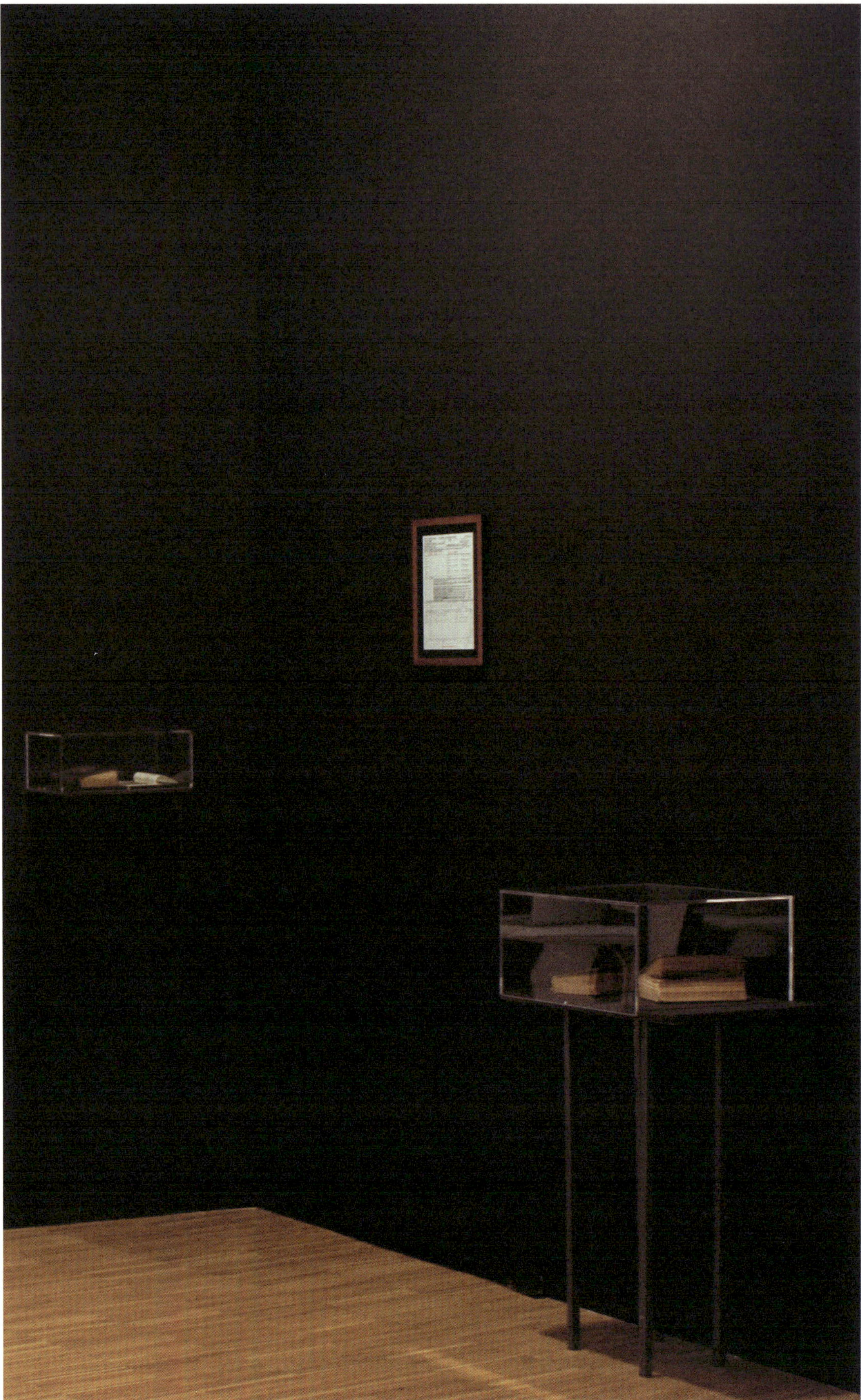

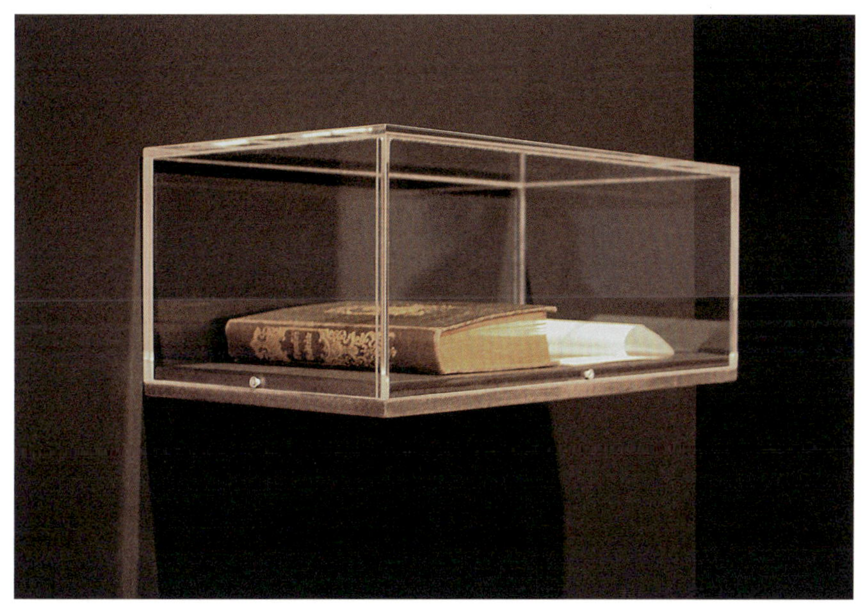

Lucile, Browning, Under the Lilacs,
installation view
Artesantander, Santander 2011

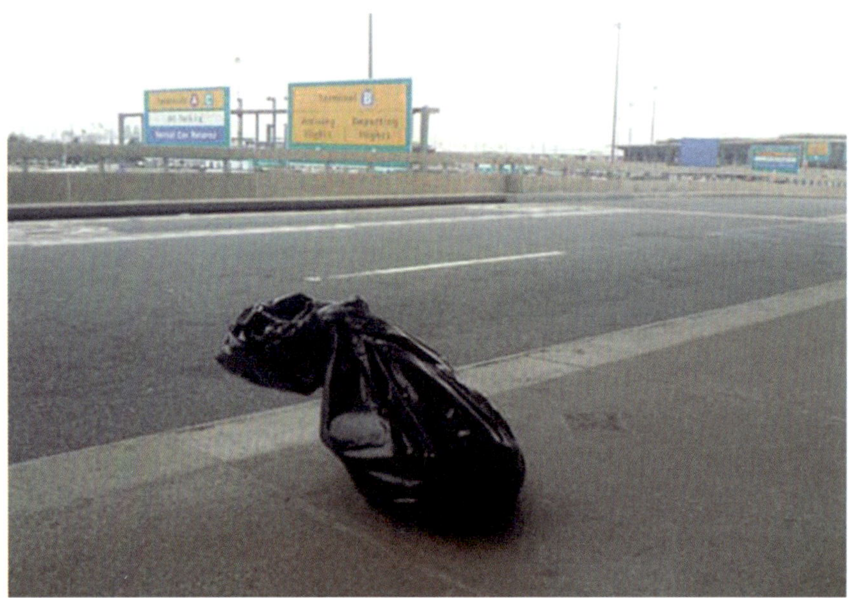

M Reheis #2809
08-12x2

PROPERTY AND EVIDENCE

The breathing book project (Thinking I'd Last Forever) had alerted the authorities at Newark Liberty Int. Airport in summer 2008. At the check-in to my return flight to Germany. FBI, CIA, TSA and the Police evacuated the entire terminal, a bomb squat flew in with a helicopter to check my suitcase. I was interrogated for hours, the breathing books were confiscated.

Three months later I was able to retrieve my belongings: I met a civilian officer in a white car at a terminal C at EWR. The books were returned to me in a black garbage bag at the curbside. All mechanisms were manipulated and each book had been signed and numbered by the officer.

EIGENTUM UND BEWEISMITTEL

Die Serie der atmenden Bücher (Thinking I'd Last Forever) alarmierte die Behörden am Newark Liberty Int. Airport im Sommer 2008. Während der Check-in-Prozedur zu meinem Rückflug nach Deutschland wurden sie entdeckt. FBI, CIA, TSA und die Polizei evakuierten aufgrund dessen den gesamten Terminal, ein Bombenentschärfungsteam kümmerte sich um meinen Koffer. Ich wurde stundenlang befragt, am Ende wurden alle atmenden Bücher konfisziert.

Erst drei Monate später erhielt ich sie zurück: Die Übergabe erfolgte durch einen Beamten in Zivil in einem weißen Auto am Terminal C. Die Bücher wurden mir in einer schwarzen Mülltüte ausgehändigt und ich selbst am Bordstein zurückgelassen. Alle Mechanismen waren zerstört, und jedes Buch war als Beweismittel sowohl nummeriert als auch durch den diensthabenden Polizisten signiert.

POLICE DEPARTMENT — PROPERTY & EVIDENCE RECEIPT — NEWARK,

1. FOUND OR RECOVERED BY	2. SECTOR	3. COMMAND	4. DISTRICT NO.	5. CENTRAL COMPLAINT NO.
P.O. M. REHEIS	317	NLIA		Court Office Use Only

6. LOCATION WHERE FOUND OR RECOVERED	7. TIME & DATE FOUND OR RECOVERED
CI CHECKPOINT _ TERMINAL C_ NEWARK AIRPORT	6/19/08 4:30 pm

8. OWNER'S NAME	9. ADDRESS & ZIP CODE	10. TELEPHONE NO.
STEFANIE EDITH KOLLATH	86 STRESEMANNSTRABE HAMBURG, GERMANY 22769	646 812 7408

11. BRIEF EXPLANATION OF FINDING OR RECOVERY:
DURING TSA SCREENING, THE OBJECTS BELOW WERE FOUND INSIDE THE SUBJECTS CARRY ON LUGGAGE AND ALSO HER CHECKED LUGGAGE.

PA ARR# N/A **PA CCR#** 08-7262

12. PRISONER (A)	C.A. NUMBER	AGE	DATE OF ARREST	13. ENVELOPE CONTROL NUMBER
ADDRESS:	CHARGES:			NARCOTICS ONLY
PRISONER (B)	C.A. NUMBER	AGE	DATE OF ARREST	ENVELOPE CONTROL NUMBER
ADDRESS:	CHARGES:			NARCOTICS ONLY
PRISONER (C)	C.A. NUMBER	AGE	DATE OF ARREST	ENVELOPE CONTROL NUMBER
ADDRESS:	CHARGES:			NARCOTICS ONLY
PRISONER (D)	C.A. NUMBER	AGE	DATE OF ARREST	ENVELOPE CONTROL NUMBER
ADDRESS:	CHARGES:			NARCOTICS ONLY

14. ITEM NO.	15. QTY.	16. EVIDENCE SOURCE	17. ARTICLE DESCRIPTION	18. ESTIMATED C. VALUE
1	1		BROWN BOOK TITLED LUCILE, ELECTRONIC DEVICE AND BATTERY COMPONENTS INSIDE EVIDENCE BAG 11506196	UNKNOWN
2	1		BROWN BOOK TITLED LONGFELLOWS POEMS, ELECTRONIC DEVICE AND BATTERY COMPON COMPONENTS INSIDE EVIDENCE BAG 11506197	UNKNOWN
3	1		GREEN BOOK TITLED IF WINTER COMES, ELECTRONIC DEVICE AND BATTERY COMPONENTS INSIDE EVIDENCE BAG 11506191	UNKNOWN
4	1		BROWN BOOK TITLED LOVE AND LIBERTY, ELECTRONIC DEVICE AND BATTERY COMPONENTS INSIDE EVIDENCE BAG 11506200	UNKNOWN
5	1		GREEN BOOK TITLED BROWNING, ELECTRONIC DEVICE AND BATTERY COMPONENT INSIDE EVIDENCE BAG 11506198	UNKNOWN
6	1		BROWN BOOK TITLED LILACS, ELECTRONIC DEVICE AND BATTERY COMPONENT INSIDE EVIDENCE BAG 11506199	UNKNOWN
7	1		BROWN BOX AND WHITE PLASTIC BAG CONTAINING CIRCUIT BOARDS, WIRES ELECTRICAL TAPE, S[illegible] BATTERIES, BATTERY TESTER INSIDE EVIDENCE BAG [illegible]	UNKNOWN
XXXXXXXX	XXXXXXX		XXXXXXXXXXXXXXXXXXXXXXXXXXXXXXXXXXXXXXXXXXXXXXXX	XXXXXXXXX

19. NARC. FIELD TEST BY:	I.D. NO	COMMAND	COCAINE - RESULTS	HEROIN - RESULTS

20. PROPERTY: ☐ ARREST-EVIDENCE ☐ FOUND ☐ DECEDENTS ☐ STOLEN ☐ PERSONAL PROPERTY OF PRISONER ( )

21. CURRENCY	JEWELRY	FURS	CLOTHING	MISCELLANEOUS	TOTAL	TOTAL NO. OF PROP. & EVID. RECEIPTS
						22 OF RECEIPTS

23. SIGNATURE & RANK OF OFFICER EXECUTING RECEIPT	I.D. NO.	COMMAND	24. SIGNATURE OF SUPERIOR RECEIVING RECEIPT	I.D. NO	COMMAND
P.O. M. REHEIS [signature]	2809	NLIA	[signature]	175	[illegible]

BELOW FOR PROPERTY ROOM USE ONLY-RECORD OF PROPERTY MOVEMENT — 25. PROPERTY LOCATION

26. PROSECUTOR'S RELEASE SENT / RECEIVED	PHOTO TAKEN BY DATE O.K. TO RELEASE ITEMS BY	27. SIGNATURE OF PROPERTY OFFICER	DATE

28. DATE	ITEM NO.	PRINT NAME	SIGNATURE	TO	SEALED YES/NO/BY	ENVELOPE NUMBER/COMMENTS
10/03/08	7	S. Edith Kollath	[signature]		no	All items RTO

I HEREBY ACKNOWLEDGE RECEIVING FROM THE NEWARK POLICE DEPARTMENT THE PROPERTY LISTED BELOW:

29. NAME	ADDRESS	ITEM NO.	DATE:

PROPERTY ROOM WORK COPY

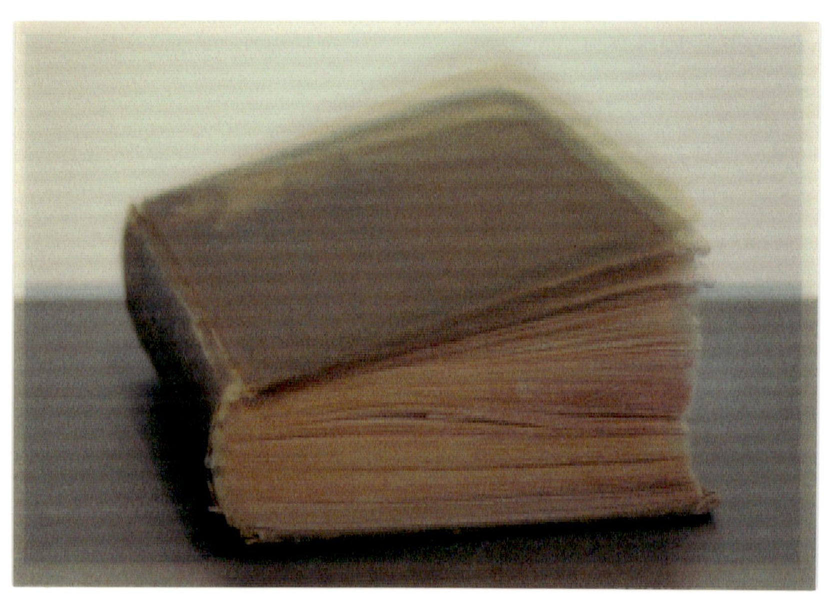

THINKING I'D LAST FOREVER

longfellow's poems, installation view, Miami 2012

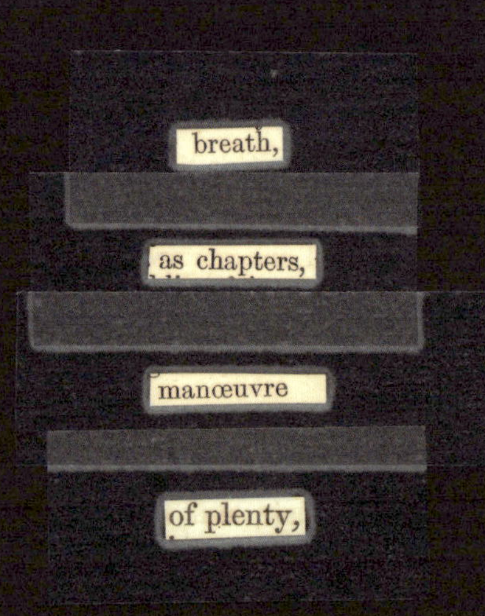
breath,
as chapters,
manœuvre
of plenty,

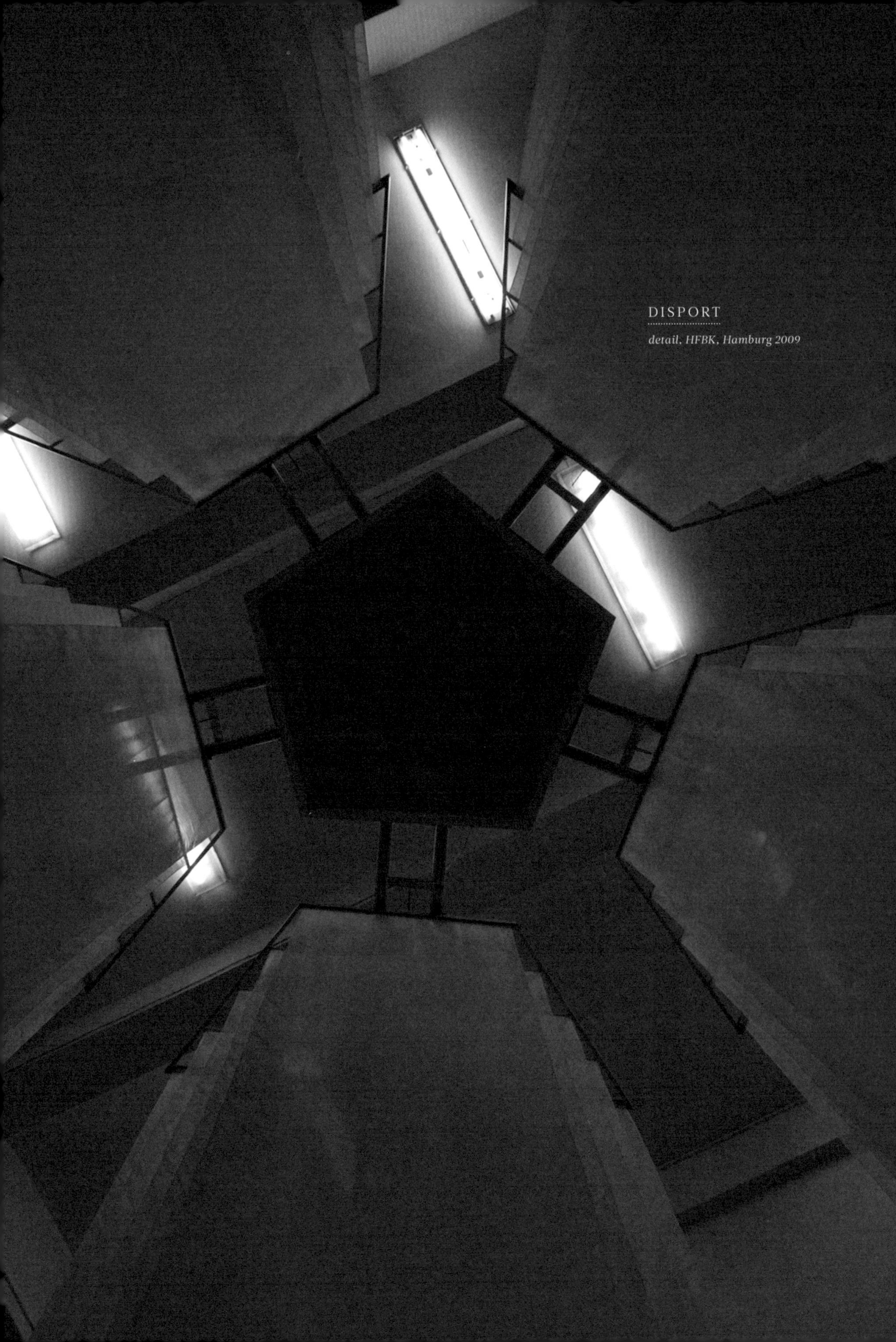

DISPORT

detail, HFBK, Hamburg 2009

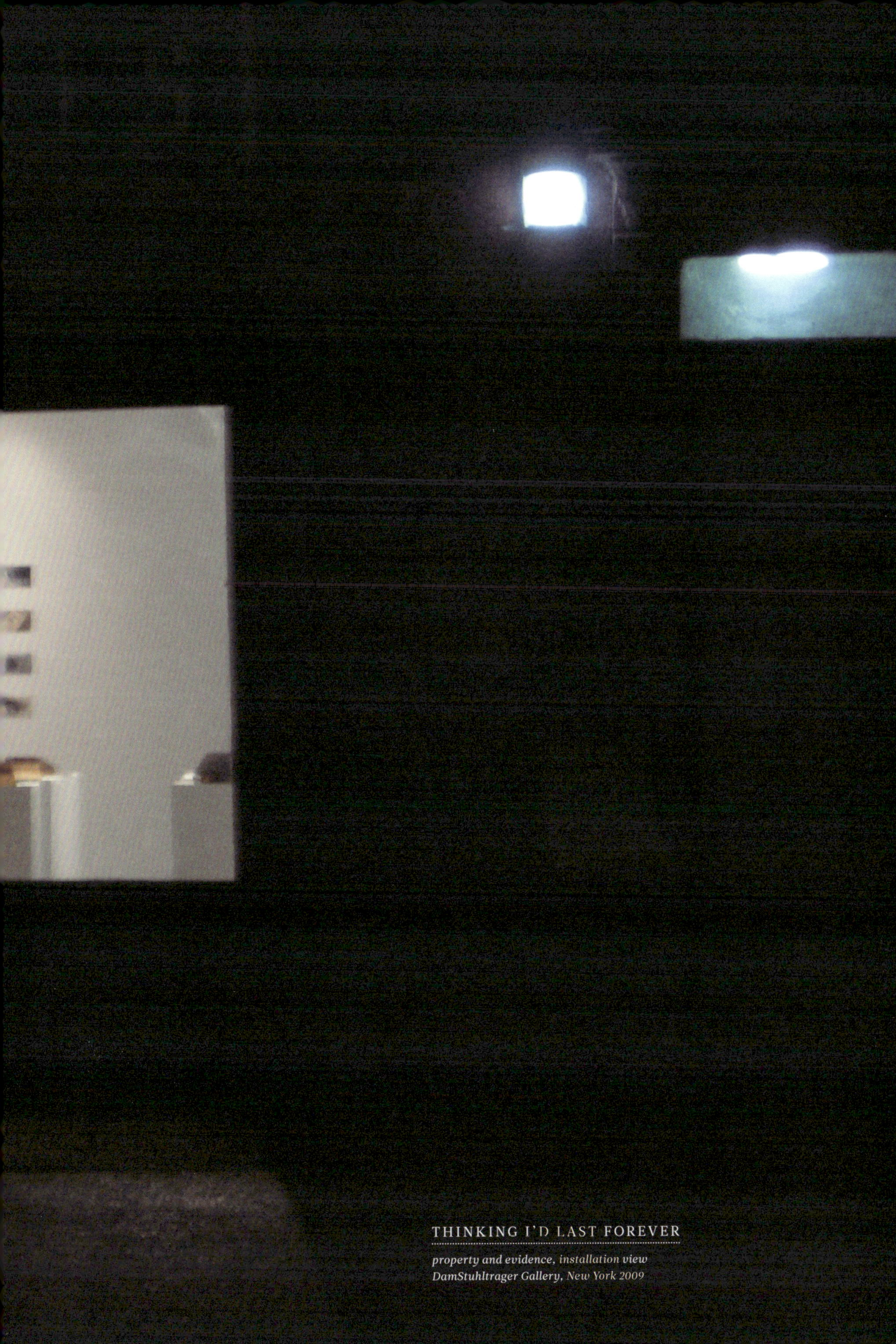

THINKING I'D LAST FOREVER

property and evidence, installation view
DamStuhltrager Gallery, New York 2009

DUETT, BIBLE AND KORAN

Smilefaucet – AIR, Fontana's, New York 2007

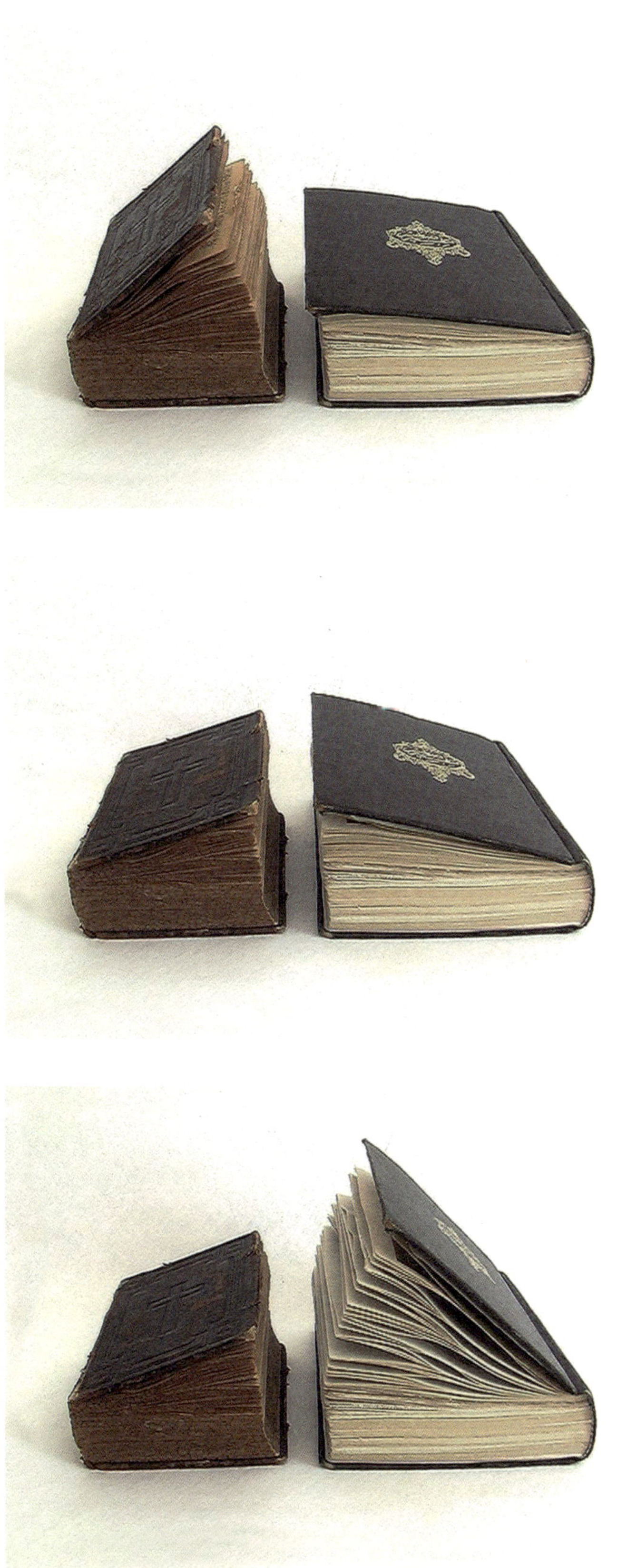

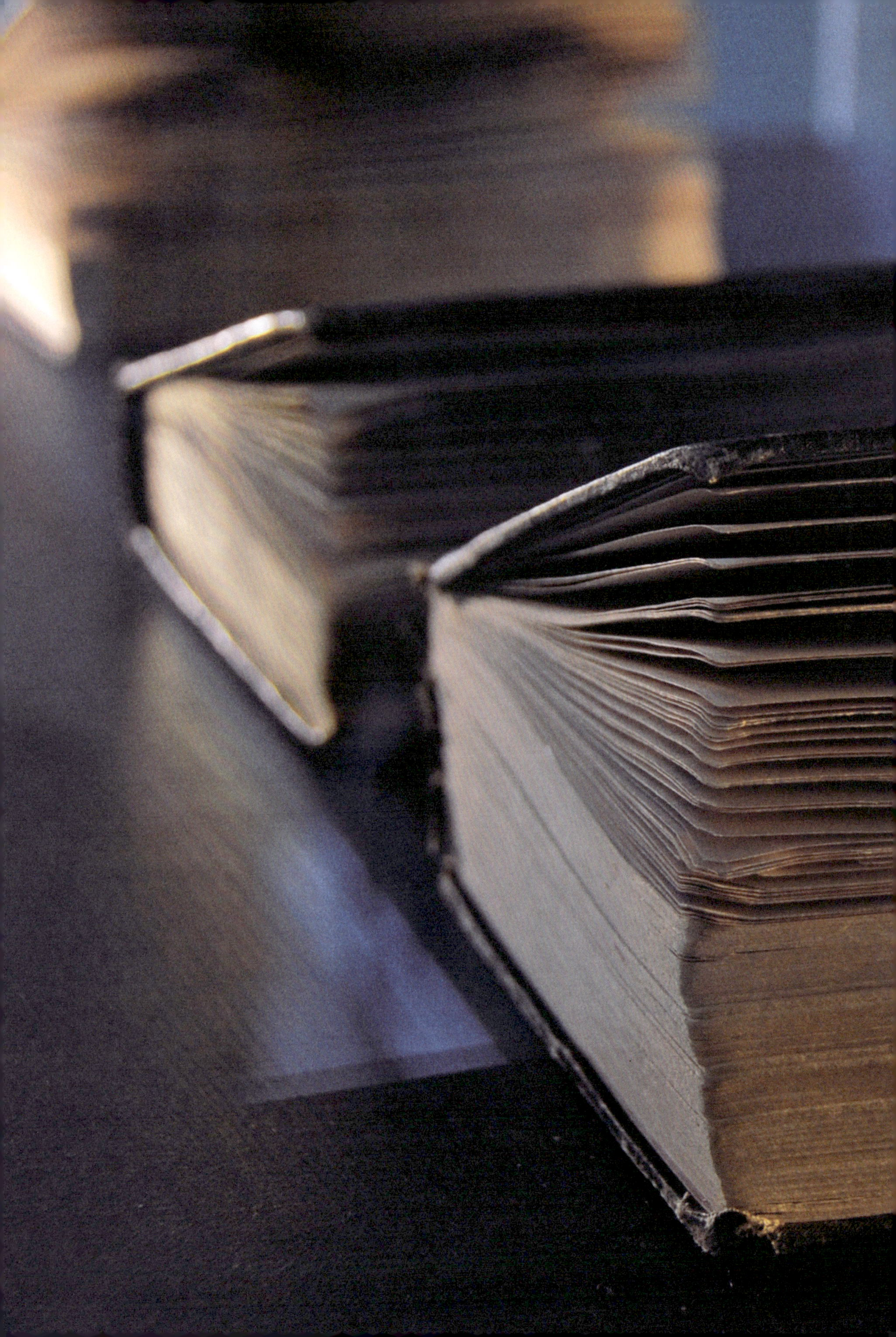

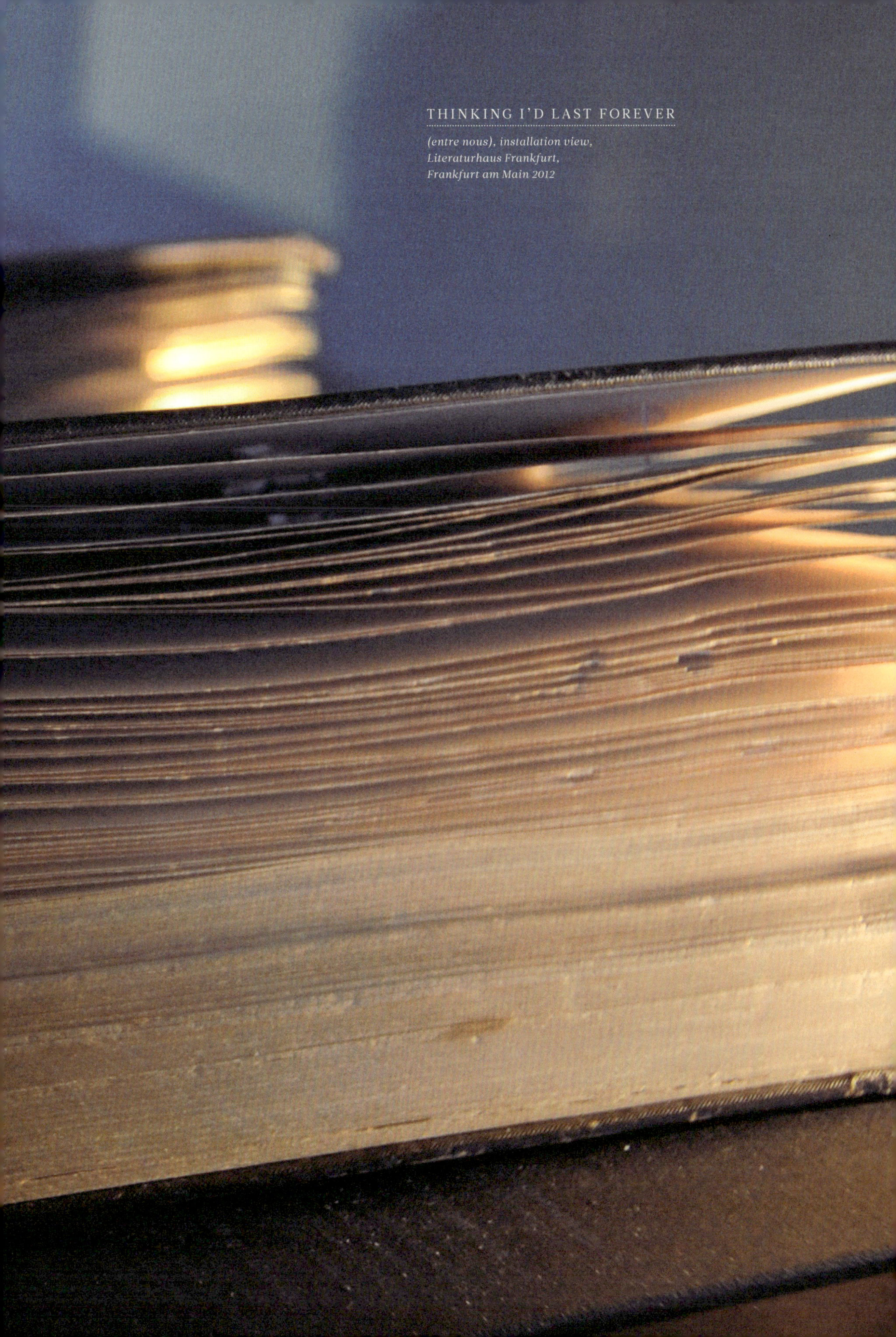

THINKING I'D LAST FOREVER

(entre nous), installation view,
Literaturhaus Frankfurt,
Frankfurt am Main 2012

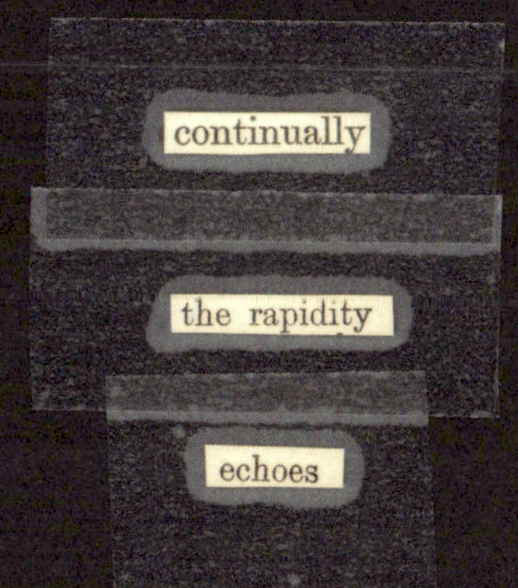
continually
the rapidity
echoes

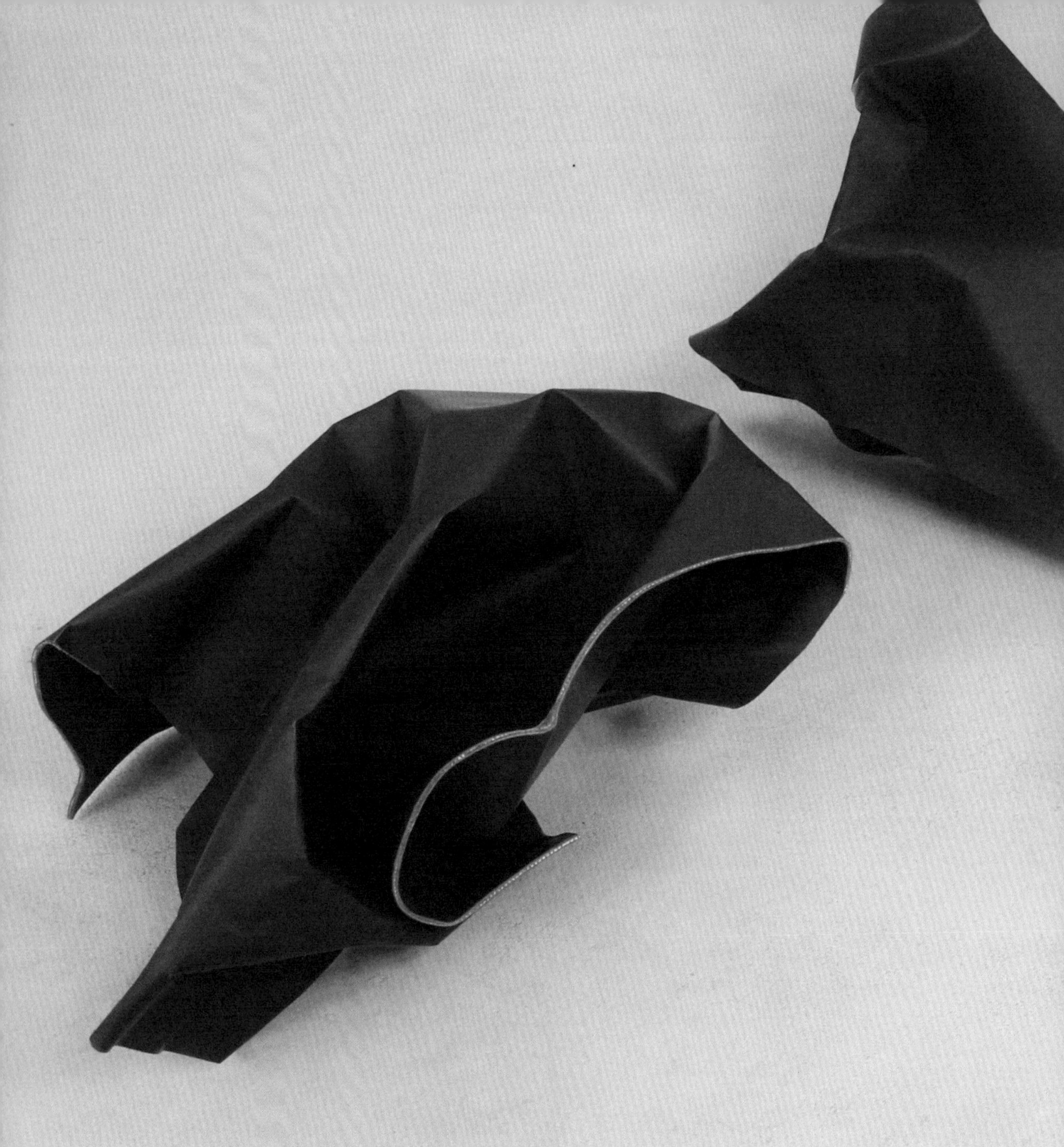

SIGH

DMY International Design Festival (Satellite), Berlin 2011

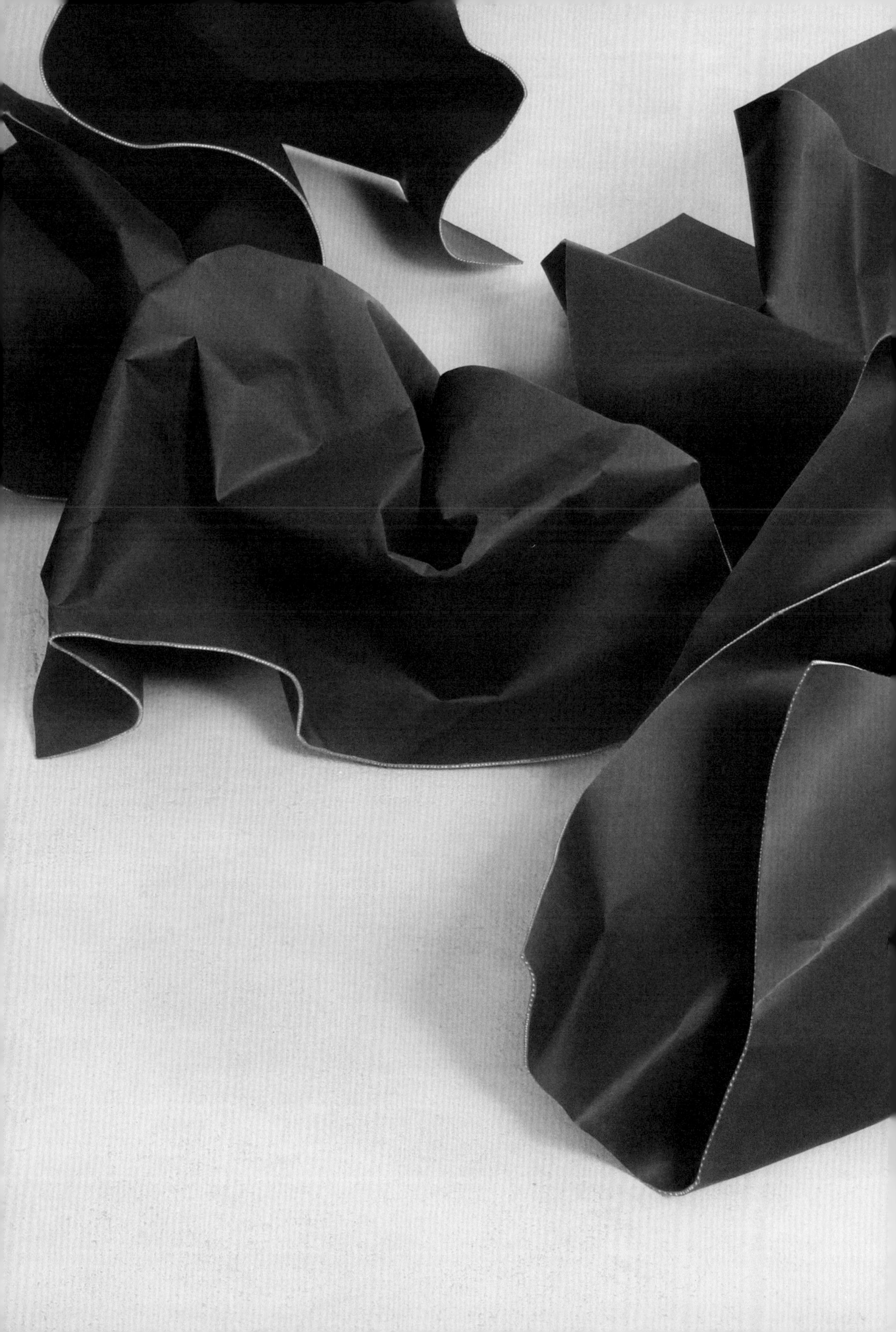

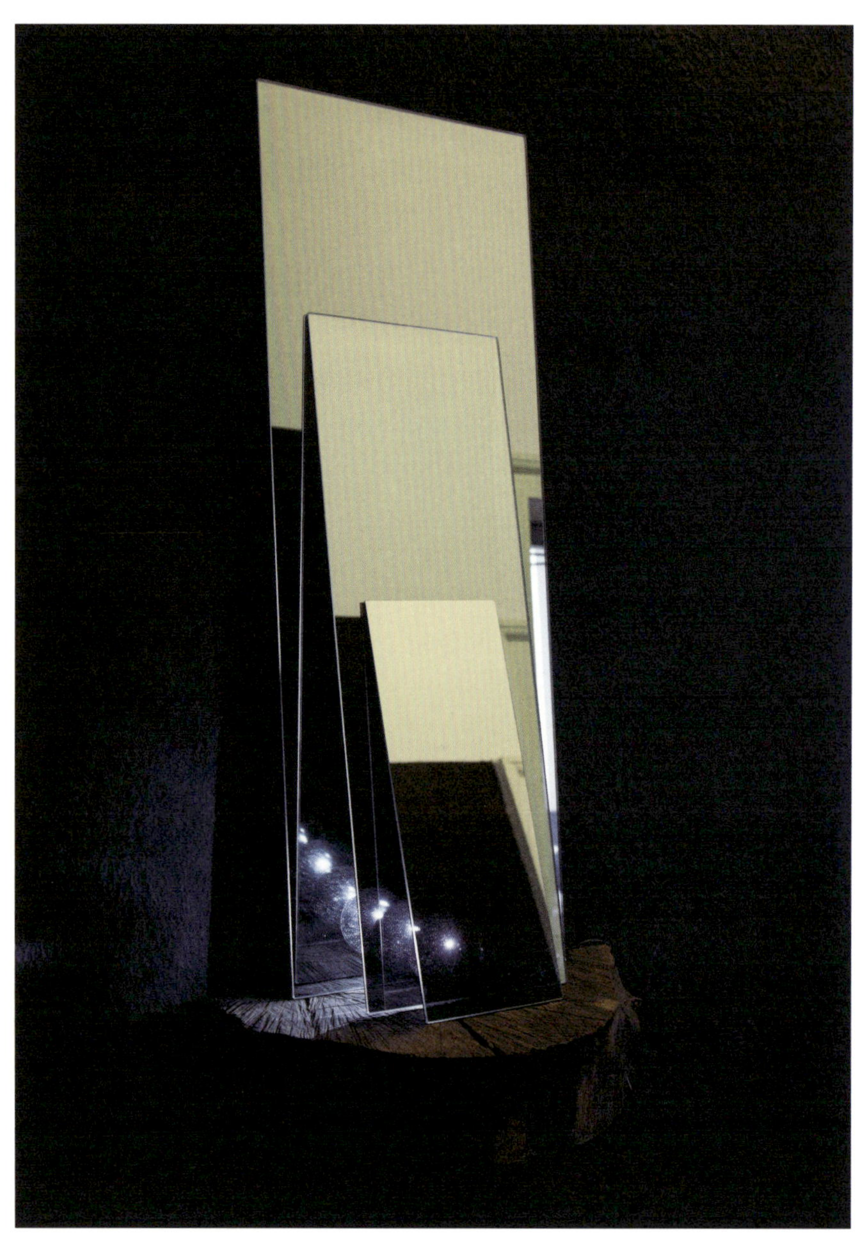

TRYING TO EXPAND THE POTENTIAL OF LOVE

in light and in gloom, installation view,
ATELIERFRANKFURT, Frankfurt am Main 2011

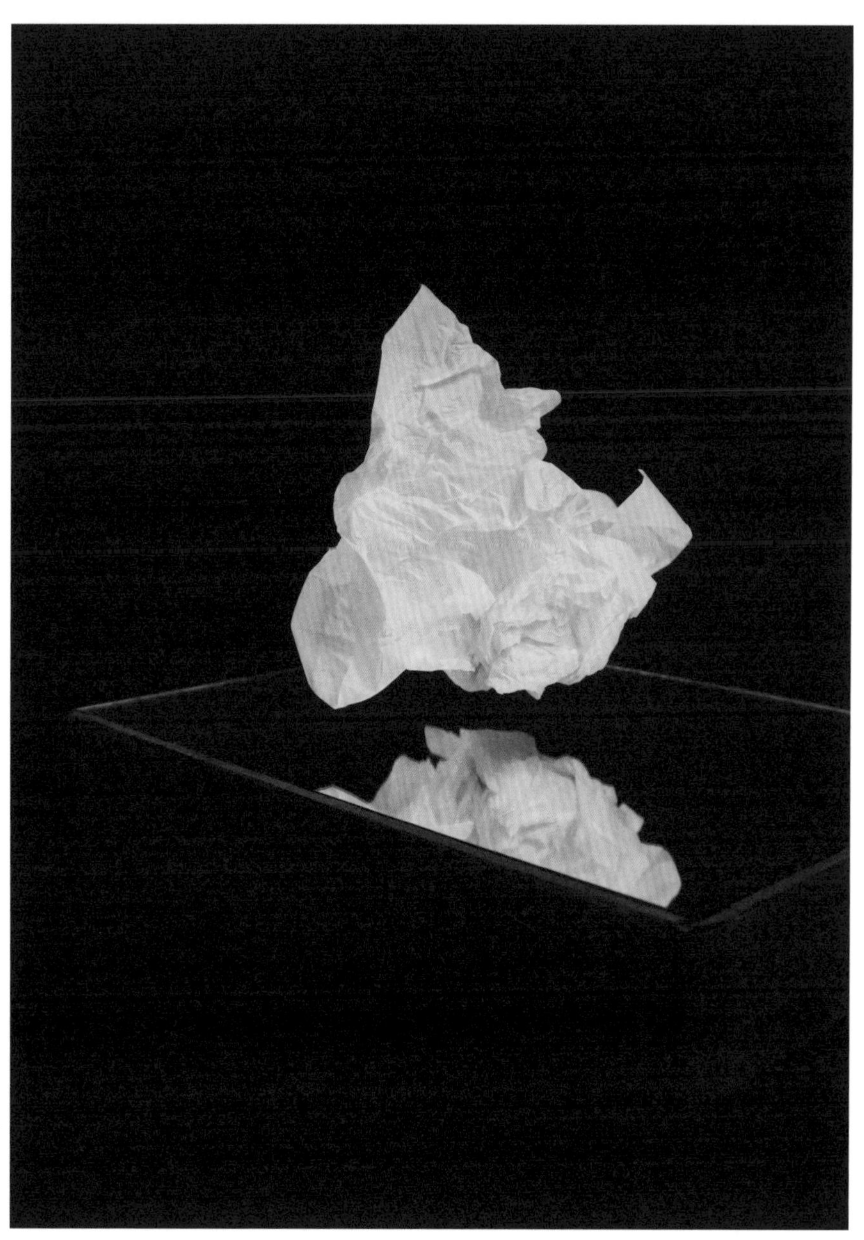

IF IT WERE A SHEET OF PAPER

in light and in gloom, installation view,
ATELIERFRANKFURT, Frankfurt am Main 2011

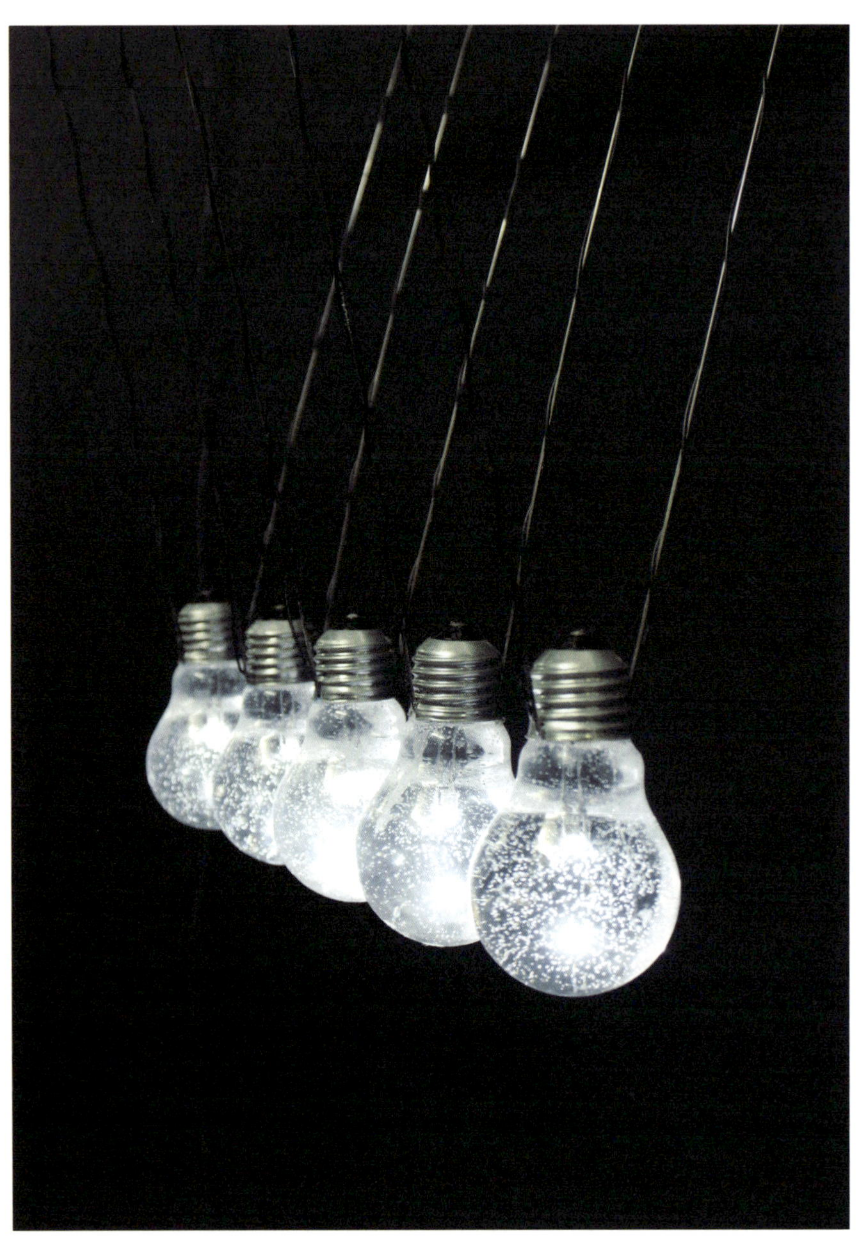

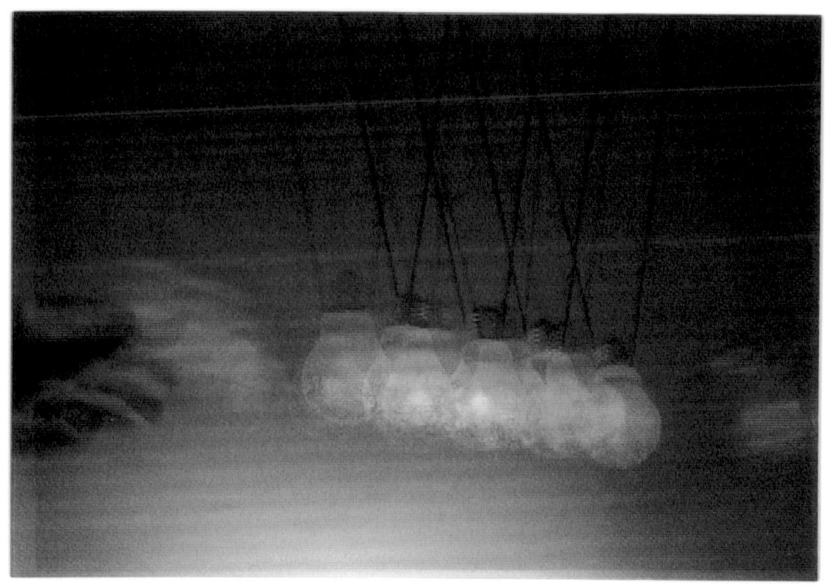

PENDULUM LUCIDUM

in light and in gloom, installation view,
ATELIERFRANKFURT, Frankfurt am Main 2011

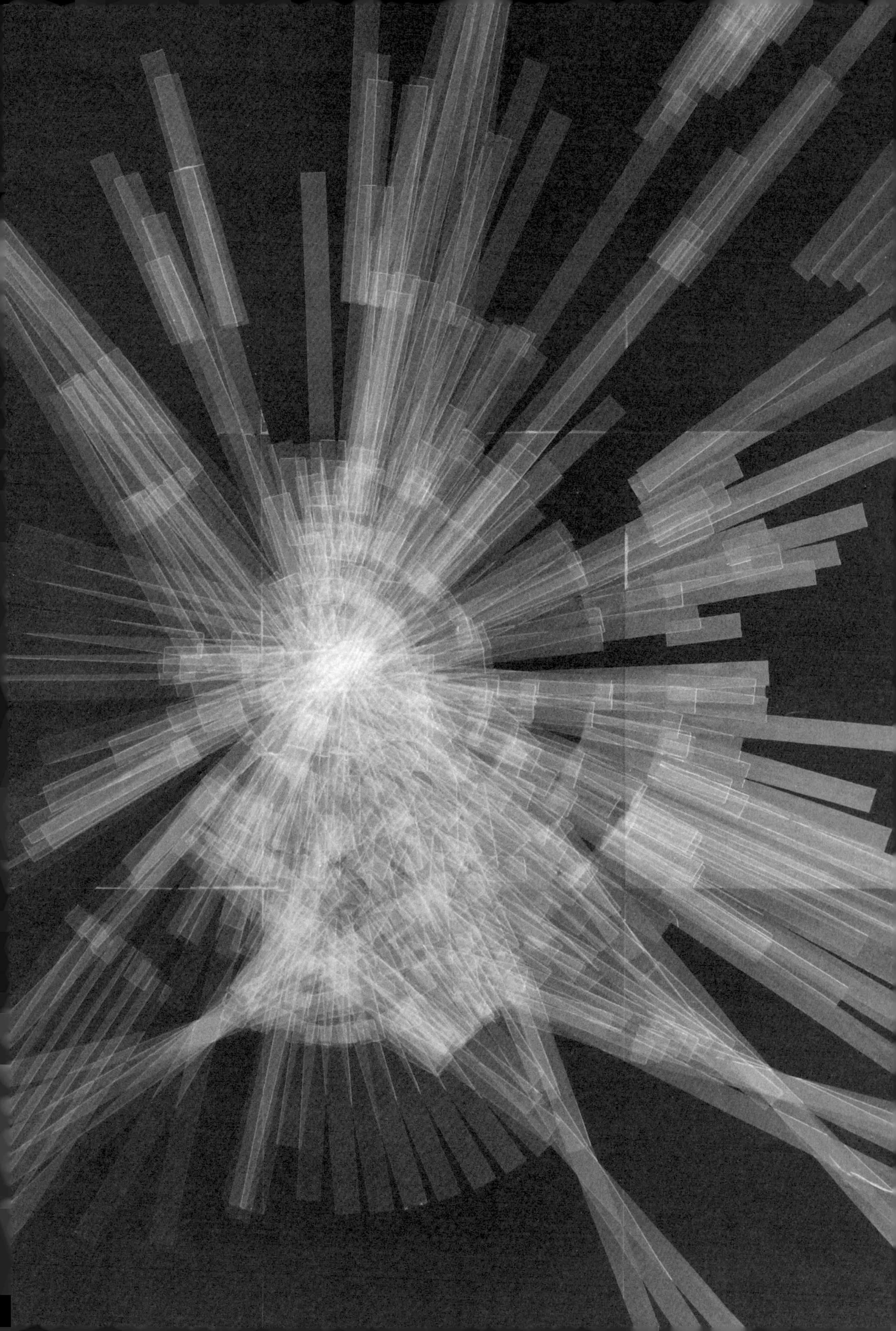

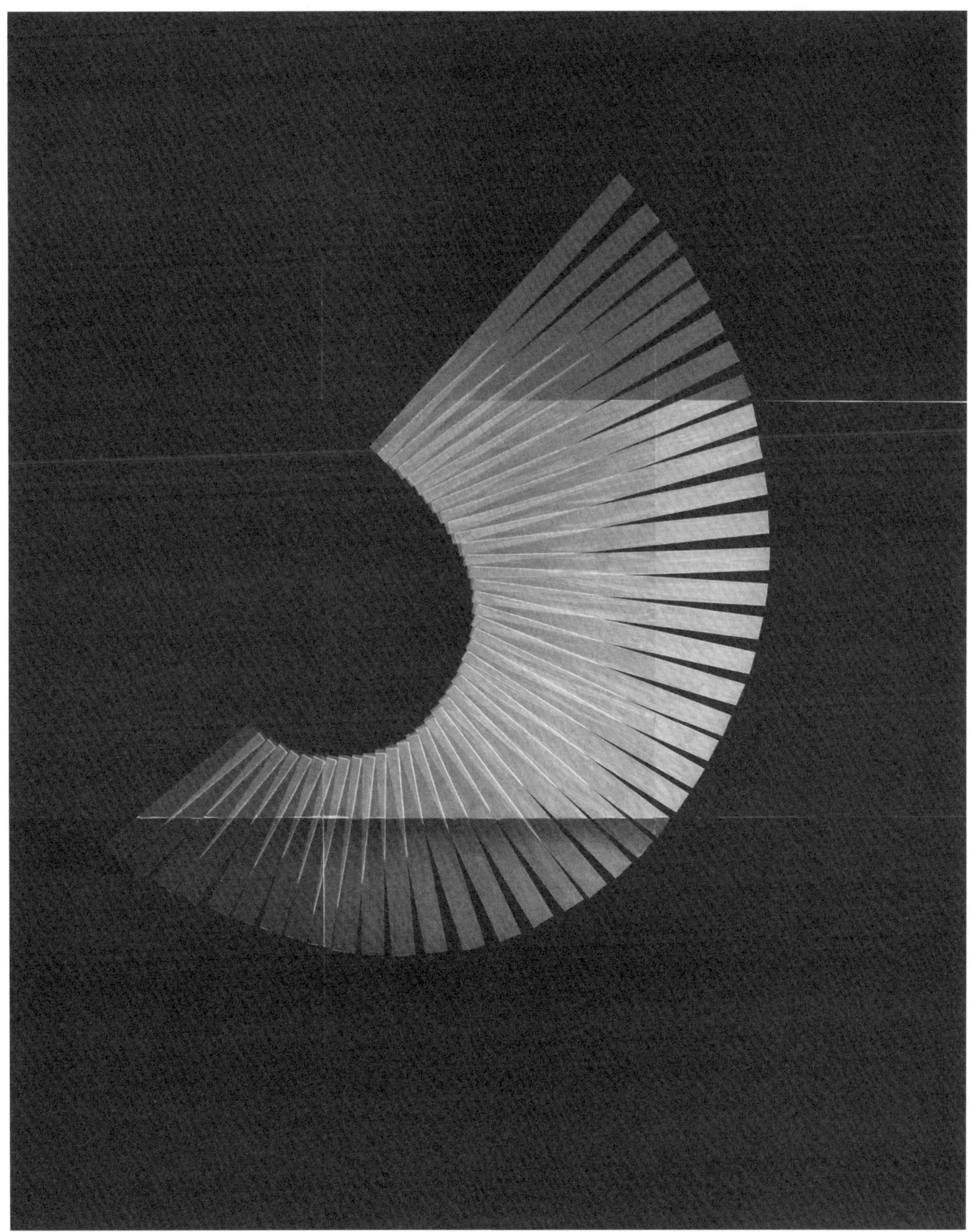

UNTITLED (TAPE)

in light and in gloom, installation view ATELIERFRANKFURT, Frankfurt am Main 2011

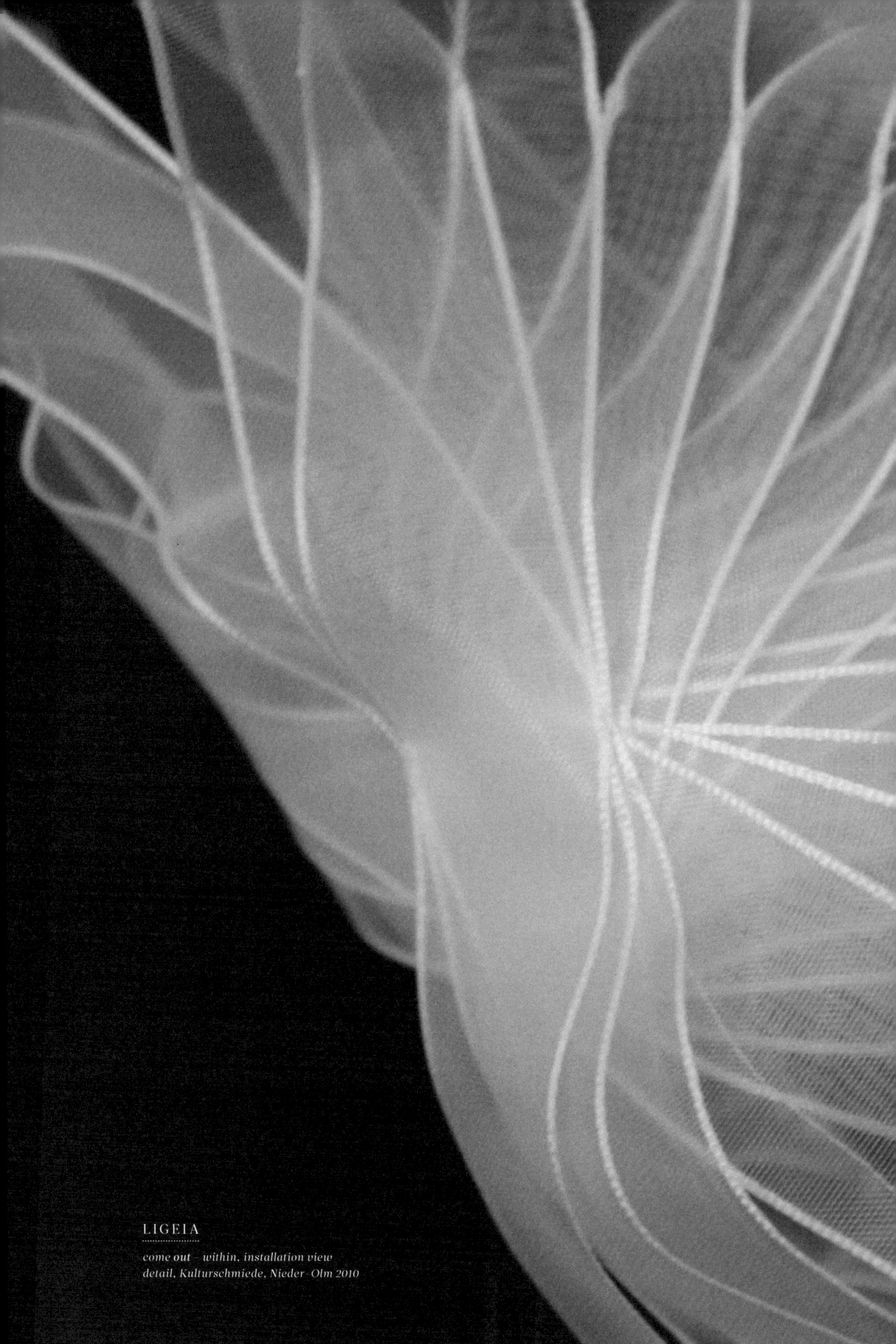

LIGEIA

*come **out** – within, installation view*
detail, Kulturschmiede, Nieder-Olm 2010

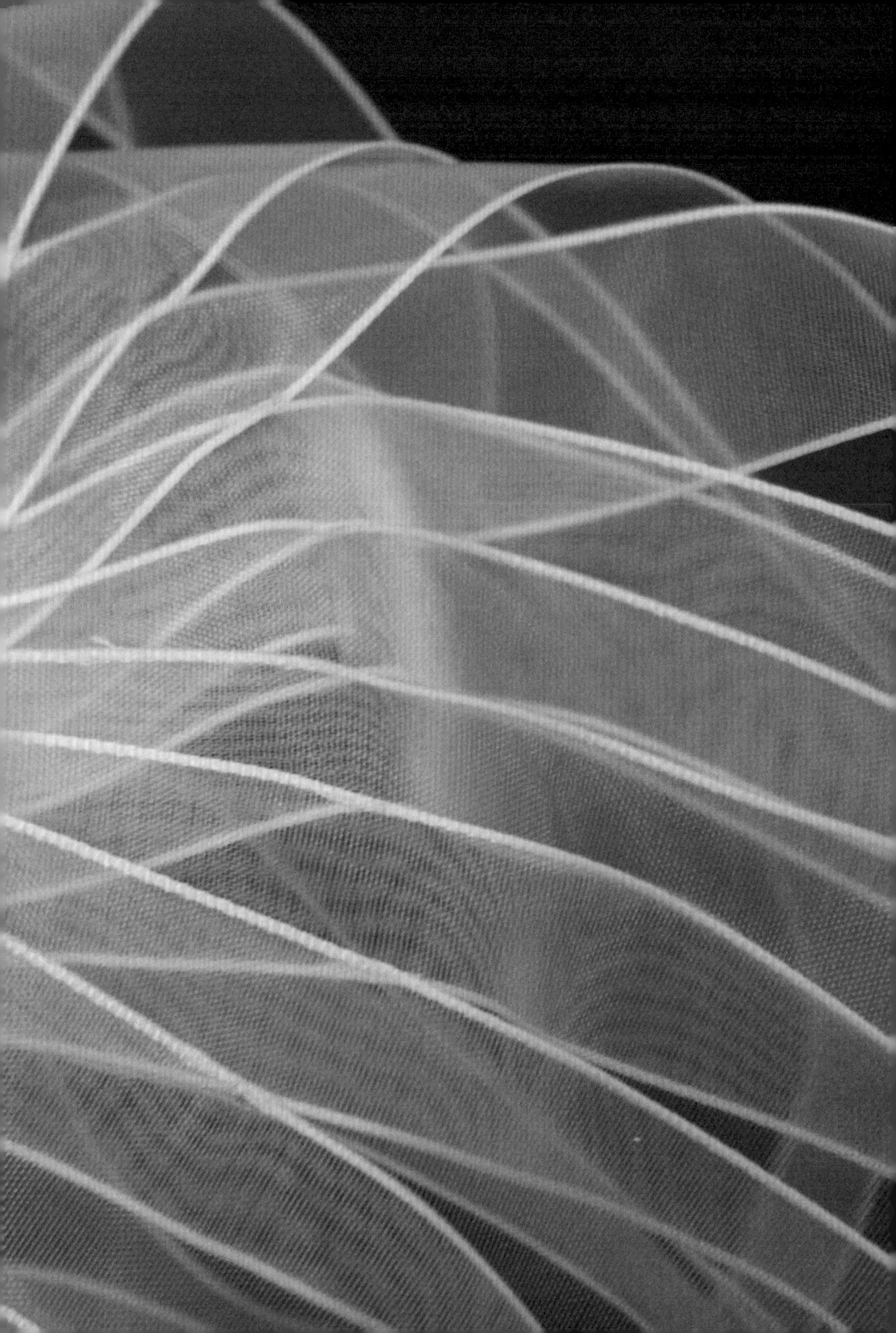

THE UBER-SEXY ENTRANCE EXPERIENCE

Apparently, the first revolving door was invented in Berlin, Germany, by a man named H. Bockhacker. Bockhacker, who was granted German patent DE 18349 on December 22, 1881, ended up calling his invention "Tür ohne Luftzug" or "Door without draft of air", a very descriptive name. Legend has it that Bockacker was originally going to call his revolving door "The Uber-Sexy Entry Experience" but was talked out of it by both his mother Chlodwiga and his aunt Engelbertha.

DIE ÜBER-SEXY EINLASS ERFAHRUNG

Die erste Drehtür wurde in Berlin von H. Bockhacker erfunden. Am 22. Dezember 1881 erhielt er das deutsche Patent DE 18349 für seine „Tür ohne Luftzug“. Der Legende nach wollte er seine Erfindung ursprünglich „Die Über-Sexy Einlass Erfahrung“ nennen, doch seine Mutter Chlodwiga und seine Tante Engelbertha redeten ihm dieses Vorhaben zugunsten eines beschreibenderen Namens aus.

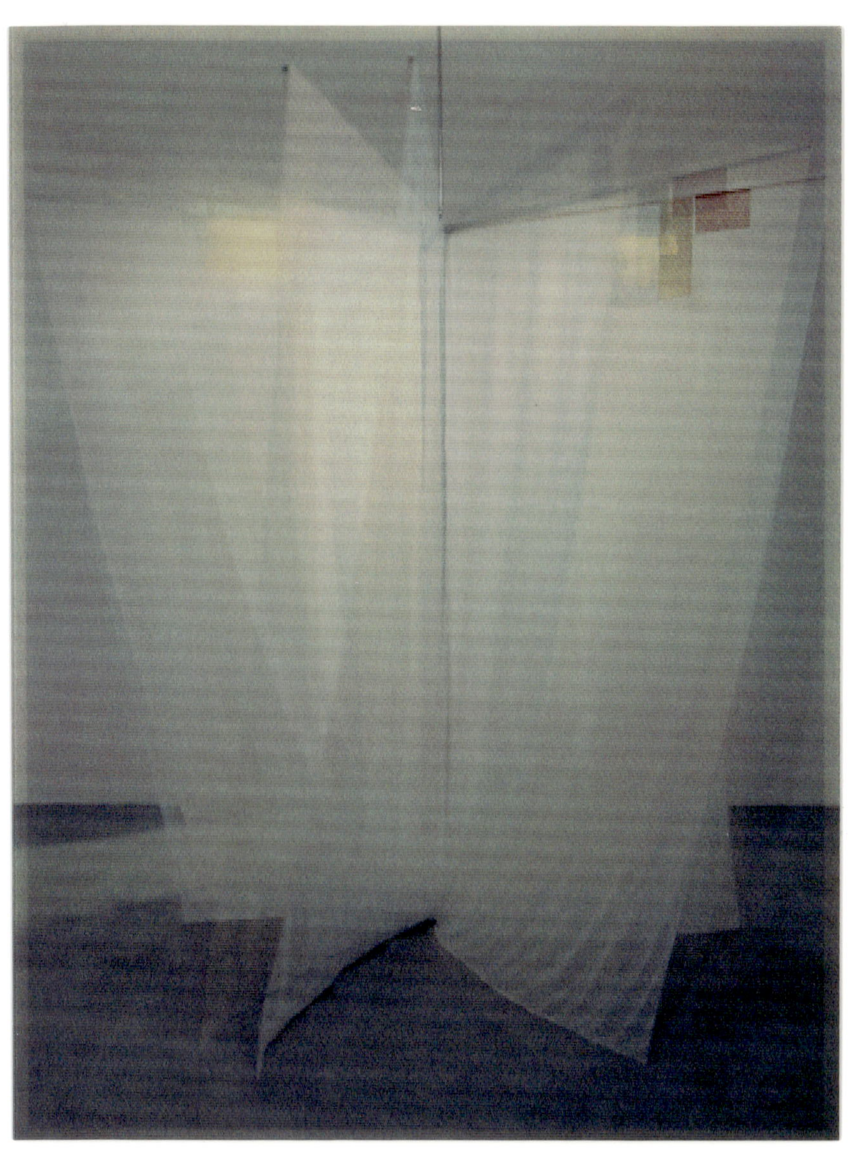

THE UBER-SEXY ENTRANCE EXPERIENCE

Balance, installation view, COLLECTIVA gallery, Berlin 2013

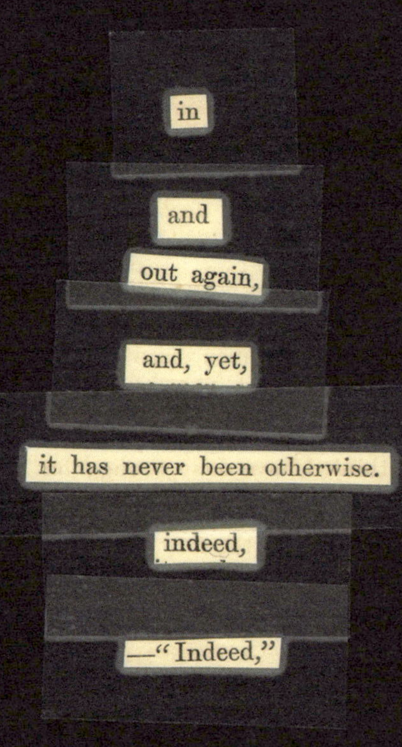
in
and
out again,
and, yet,
it has never been otherwise.
indeed,
—"Indeed,"

»DIE POESIE DES IMMATERIELLEN. EDITH KOLLATHS IMAGINATIONEN VON BEWEGTEM«

VON CHRISTINA GRAMMATIKOPOULOU

Die Bilder, die sich aus der Imagination von Bewegtem ergeben,
werden sich entweder verflüchtigen oder kristallisieren.
Wir müssen sie zwischen den
beiden Polen dieser rastlosen Ambivalenz erfassen.

GASTON BACHELARD[1]

Die mäandernden Bahnen eines Lufthauchs bilden Wolken aus Dampf, liebkosen die Falten eines Tuches, gleiten in die Seiten alter Bücher, erfüllen Körper mit der lebenspendenden Kraft des Atems und verlassen sie wieder, um weitere Körper und Räume zu erkunden.

Es ist ein Werk offener Möglichkeiten, Ausdruck von Energie und Vergänglichkeit, das Edith Kollath geschaffen hat.

Fasziniert vom Nichtsichtbaren und Immateriellen macht sie ebendiese zu strukturellen Elementen ihrer fragilen Objekte und Installationen. Durch sanfte Bewegungen und Klänge werden ihre Arbeiten lebendig und beginnen zu atmen. Es ist ein freier, ungehinderter Atemfluss, der von diesen Werken ausgeht, ein sanfter Hauch zu einem Zustand der inneren Ruhe und Meditation.

Kollath verfügt über eine breite Palette visueller Ausdrucksformen – von Video über Skulpturen bis hin zu Installationen, von abstrakten Formen bis hin zu konkreten Objekten und menschlichen Körpern –, immer geprägt von einer minimalistischen Eleganz und ruhigen Eloquenz.

Ebendiese Elemente sind es, die ***BW1*** (2006) prägen. Hier eröffnet die Kamera den Blick auf eine mit Wasser gefüllte Badewanne. Das Wasser ist beinahe unbewegt, nur eine leichte Kräuselung an der Oberfläche ist zu sehen. Wenn es dann abläuft, enthüllt es einen weiblichen Torso, der sich mit der Bewegung des Atems hebt und senkt. Das Licht, das auf ihren Unterleib gerichtet ist, bietet eine Offenbarung des

1 Gaston Bachelard. *Air and Dreams, An Essay on the Imagination of Movement*, Dallas: The Dallas Institute, 1988 (1943), S. 13. (Dieses Zitat wurde übersetzt.)

„Ursprungs der Welt". Das strukturelle und konzeptionelle Zentrum der Komposition ist jedoch der sich sanft hebende und senkende Bauchnabel, der die Aufmerksamkeit des Betrachters auf die Atmung als die wichtigste Handlung in diesem Video lenkt.

Der Atem als harmonisierendes Instrument und Mittel der Kommunikation ist das zentrale Thema im Video ***in between*** (2007), in dem ein Mann und eine Frau ihren Atem austauschen, dargestellt durch Rauch, der rhythmisch von einem Mund zum anderen fließt und die Protagonisten in einen Zustand der Ausgeglichenheit und Zufriedenheit versetzt, wie man an ihren Gesichtern erkennen kann. Den Atem des anderen zu spüren ist ein Zeichen von Intimität, wie nur Menschen sie erleben, die sich nahestehen. Zu einem gewissen Grad aber teilen wir alle die Luft zum Atmen miteinander und mit unserer Umwelt, wie Luce Irigaray schreibt: „[Zu atmen] bedeutet, mit der Welt, die mich umgibt, und mit der Gemeinschaft, die in ihr lebt, zu teilen."[2]

Auch in Kollaths Werken jenseits der Videoleinwand umgibt den Betrachter dieser Lufthauch. In der Installation ***again, again*** (2009) steigt vor einem schwarzen Hintergrund eine grauweiße Wolke auf, die sich dann im Raum verteilt, sich mit dem Atem der Besucher verbindet und so zu einer gemeinsamen visuellen und körperlichen Erfahrung wird. Gleichzeitig verändert diese Wolke immer wieder ihre Form und regt so die Fantasie des Betrachters an. Es ist eine Konstruktion, die ein fragiles und vergängliches Bild mithilfe des Zufalls und eines physikalischen Phänomens sichtbar macht.

In ***nothing will ever be the same*** (2009) wird der Zufall zum ausschlaggebenden Faktor. Bei dieser Installation wird ein transparentes Tuch durch einen automatischen Mechanismus immer wieder in die Höhe gehoben, von wo es dann zu Boden gleitet. Diese repetitive, rhythmische Bewegung führt jedes Mal zu einem anderen visuellen Ergebnis. Auf diese Weise wird das Tuch zu einer Skulptur, die sich

---

2 Irigaray, Luce. „From The Forgetting of Air to To Be two", in: Nancy Holland und Patricia Huntington, *Feminist Interpretations of Martin Heidegger*, Pennsylvania 2001, S. 309.

ständig bewegt und verändert und dabei aufgrund des Luftwiderstands und der Schwerkraft die unterschiedlichsten Formen annimmt. Während das Tuch fällt und sich wieder hebt, dringt Luft in seine Falten und gibt so seiner fließenden Gestalt eine organische Körperlichkeit. Auf diese Weise wird das Tuch lebendig, wie eine Tänzerin in einem leeren Raum, die sanft auf den harten Boden hinabsinkt. Beim nächsten Fall wird das Tuch eine neue Choreografie „improvisieren", eine andere Flugbahn wählen und an einer anderen Stelle landen. In dieser Bewegung „wird jeder Lufthauch zum Leben erweckt. Es ist ein Stück aus dem Körper der Luft, das einst lebendig war, ein ätherisches Gewebe, das eine Seele umhüllen wird".[3]

Fließender in ihrer Bewegung und ebenso lyrisch in ihrer Sprache, lädt die Installation ***disport*** (2009) den Betrachter ein, in eine fünfeckige Zelle aus Stoffbahnen zu treten, die sanft auf und zu schwingen, während das Licht im gleichen Rhythmus zwischen hell und dunkel changiert. Hier präsentiert die Künstlerin einen abgegrenzten Raum, der zugleich die Fähigkeit besitzt, sich zu öffnen, und der im ständigen, semipermeablen Austausch zu seiner Umgebung steht, wie ein lebendiger Körper, der atmet und sich in den Raum hineinbewegt. Indem die Installation den gesamten Körper anspricht, nicht nur die Augen und den Verstand, lädt sie den Betrachter ein, sich seiner eigenen Körperlichkeit gewahr zu werden und sich einem Zustand gesteigerten Bewusstseins seiner selbst und seiner Umgebung zu überlassen. Das Visuelle und das Körperliche stehen dabei im Einklang.

Diese beiden Elemente, ergänzt durch „logos" (das Wort), finden sich auch in ***thinking I'd last forever*** (2008). Die Serie besteht aus antiquarischen Büchern, Klassikern der Weltliteratur, die mithilfe von Mikroprozessoren in ihrem Innern „atmen" dürfen. Auf diese Weise erhält jedes Buch neben seinem jeweils individuellen Erscheinungsbild und Inhalt auch einen eigenen Atemrhythmus, wobei es langsam seinen Deckel hebt und sich öffnet, als würde jemand durch die Seiten

---

3 Bachelard 1988, S. 230.

blättern. In einer Zeit, in der gedruckte Bücher obsolet zu werden drohen, gelingt es Edith Kollath, gebrauchten Ausgaben ein neues Leben einzuhauchen, indem sie das klassische Format des gebundenen Buches mit moderner Technik kombiniert. Diese Bücher, die im Laufe ihres Lebens den Atem unzähliger Leser in sich aufgenommen haben, geben diesen nun weiter an den Betrachter der Installation. Mit ihren sanften Bewegungen laden sie uns Heutige ein, das Wissen und die Fantasiewelten zu erkunden, die sich in diesen Seiten verbergen und die noch immer von Bedeutung sind, auch wenn sie vor langer Zeit schon in ihre endgültige Form gebracht wurden.

Von dieser „endgültigen Form" zurück zur anfänglichen Idee: ***sigh*** (2011) zollt dem kreativen Prozess und all den Formen, die eine Idee annimmt, bevor sie ihren endgültigen Zustand erreicht, Tribut: Es ist zerknülltes Papier auf dem Fußboden, das durch die Hand, die es fortwirft, willkürliche Formen bildet, bevor es endgültig entsorgt wird. In der Installation wird zerknülltes schwarzes Papier zu dauerhaften Skulpturen plastifiziert und somit zu Artefakten erhoben. Mit ihren eleganten Formen, die sich gegen die weiße Ausstellungsfläche abheben, werden sie zu einem gemeinschaftlichen Akt von spontaner Geste und bewusster Konservierung.

If it were a sheet of paper (2011) wurde von denselben Kräften geformt. Ein zerknülltes Stück Seidenpapier schwebt über einem Spiegel wie eine Wolke, deren Bild im Wasser reflektiert wird. Die offensichtliche Missachtung jeglicher physikalischer Gesetze weckt ein Gefühl der Neugierde und Verspieltheit im Betrachter, der versucht ist herauszufinden, ob er das Seidenpapier mit seinem Atem in Schwingung bringen kann. Gleichzeitig erzeugt die Negierung der Schwerkraft, der stetige Aufschub des drohenden Falls ein Energiefeld zwischen dem Papier und seiner Spiegelung.

Ein Konservieren von Energie, ein Verharren in Reglosigkeit und eine rhythmische Bewegung: ***pendulum lucidum*** (2011) ist eine Interpretation des Newtonpendels mit bearbeiteten Glühbirnen. Hier finden zwei voneinander getrennte Pendelbewegungen statt: der sanfte Wechsel von hell und dunkel, indem die Glühbirnen langsam aufleuchten und wieder verlöschen, und das Schwingen der Birnen, das von einer äußeren Kraft in Bewegung gesetzt werden muss. Auf diese Weise wird das Werk zu einem Scharnier zwischen einem werkinternen Rhythmus und der Interaktion mit der Umwelt.

Auch ***trying to expand the potential of love I can give*** (2011) basiert auf dieser Verknüpfung, in der flüchtige Reflexionen, Lichtwellen und eine das alles umgebende Dunkelheit interagieren. In dieser Installation wurden semitransparente Spionspiegel wie schützend vor eine Lichtquelle auf einem Stück Holz montiert. Das sanft zwischen hell und dunkel oszillierende Licht erschafft zahlreiche Reflexionen zwischen den einzelnen Spiegeln und lässt gleichzeitig die fragmentierte Spiegelung des Betrachters verschwinden oder klar hervortreten. Es ist eine Reflexion, die sich auflöst, um den Blick auf das freizugeben, was dahinterliegt, so wie das Betrachten eines Gesichts häufig die psychologischen Tiefen hinter diesem offenbart. Auf diese Weise bilden die Spiegel eine Grenze, bei der der Ausstellungsraum ins Unendliche übergeht und Äußerlichkeiten verschwinden, um den Blick auf das Verborgene freizugeben.

In gewisser Weise scheint Edith Kollath Formen entstehen zu lassen, die sich verselbstständigen und in den Raum hineinwachsen; deutlich zu sehen in ***ligeia*** (2010), einer fragilen Konstruktion aus Federstahl und Textilband, die in ihre Umgebung hineinzuschweben scheint wie eine Unterwassergestalt, sowie Kollaths Tape-Reihe ***untitled (tape)*** (2010 – 11), bei der das transparente Klebeband vor dem dunklen Hintergrund zu tanzen scheint wie in einer verborgenen Strömung, die die einzelnen Streifen auseinandertreibt und wieder zusammenführt. Auch ihre abstrakten Zeichnungen ***lines and space*** (2009) zeigen diesen Drang, sich zu bewegen, wenn sie über das Papier kriechen und sich in seinen schwarzen Tiefen verlieren. Bei ***untitled (tape-text)*** (2011) folgt das Klebeband einer gewissen Struktur – immer ein Streifen nach dem anderen – und bildet so ein Gedicht; dessen Wörter scheinen willkürlich ausgeatmet worden zu sein, werden jedoch durch Wiederholung und Variation in eine visuell und literarisch sinnhafte

Struktur eingeflochten, die einen Einblick in Kollaths Arbeit bietet, wie ein Band, das Luftbewegungen, Materialveränderungen und Wechsel von Licht und Dunkelheit zusammenhält. Tatsächlich lässt die Beständigkeit, mit der die Künstlerin feine geschwungene Linien, Folien und dunkle Hintergründe verwendet, ihr Werk trotz der vielfältigen Medien einheitlich wirken.

Edith Kollaths „Imaginationen von Bewegtem" erschaffen filigrane Bilder, die im Nichtstofflichen und Vergänglichen verwurzelt sind, die hinausschweben und so den Betrachter auch körperlich erreichen. Ihre Arbeiten wollen mit allen Sinnen erfahren werden, sie bleiben in Erinnerung, trotz ihrer Vergänglichkeit. Entführt in eine Welt sanfter Bewegungen und sich wiederholender Klänge, rhythmischen Atems und sanfter Lichter, findet der Beobachter einen Zugang zu intellektueller Auseinandersetzung, kollektiver Kommunikation und innerer Balance.

Auf diese Weise reicht Edith Kollaths Werk über die Grenzen ihrer Ausstellung hinaus: Es wird zu einer bleibenden Erfahrung, die noch lange nachschwingt.

BARCELONA, FEBRUAR 2013

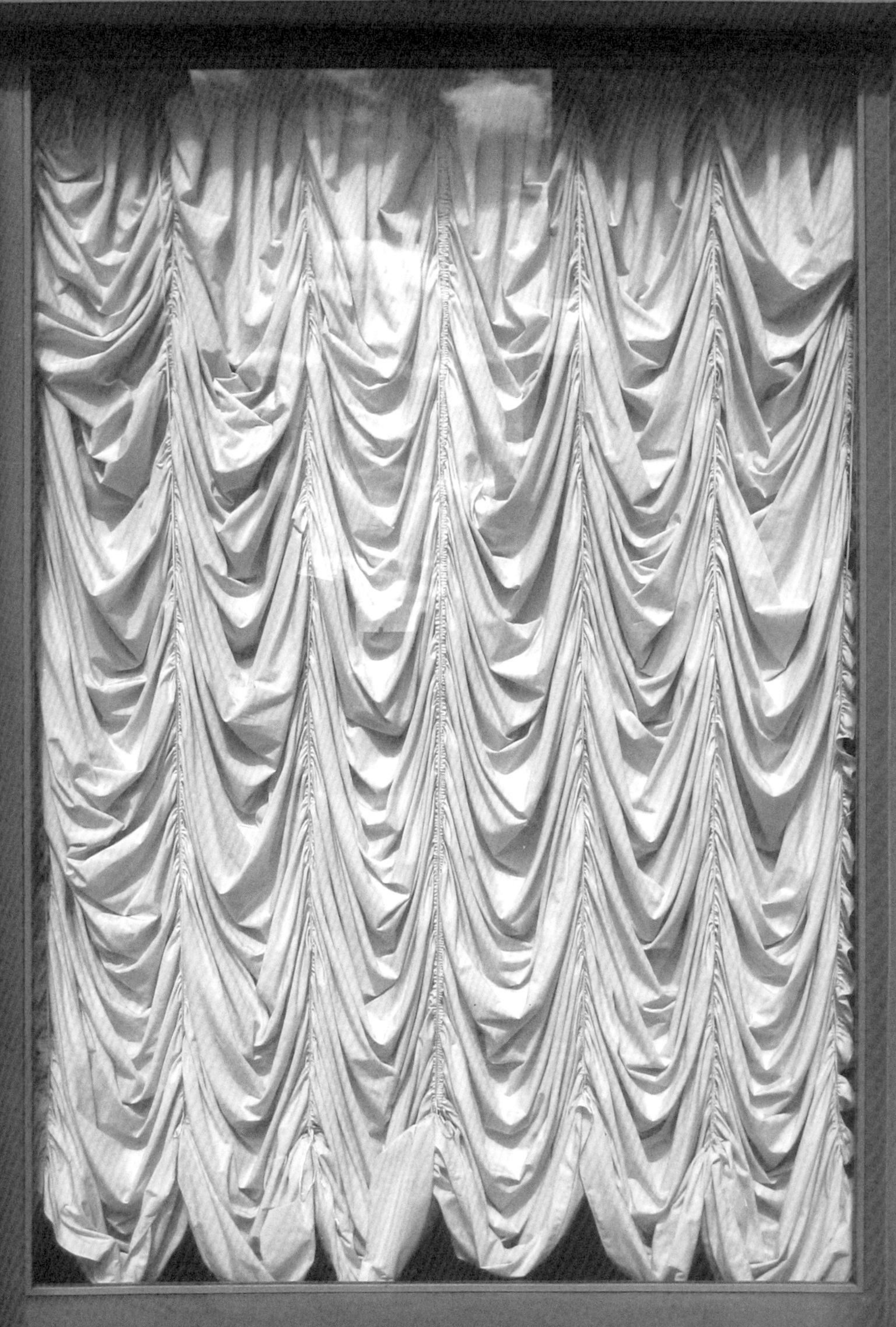

PHOTOGRAPH

Milano 2010

EDITH KOLLATH

BORN 1977 IN EUTIN, GERMANY

LIVES AND WORKS IN FRANKFURT AM MAIN AND BERLIN

EDUCATION

2009 ***MFA,*** University of Fine Arts, HFBK Hamburg, Germany
Department of Time Related Media and Sculpture

2003 ***MFA,*** University of Applied Sciences, Hamburg, Germany
Department of Textile-, Fashion- & Costume Design

2000 ***Aristotelous University of Thessaloniki,*** Greece,
Department of Fine Arts

2000 ***BA Fashion Design,*** University of Applied Sciences, Hamburg, Germany

1999 ***Central Saint Martins College of Arts and Design,*** London, Great Britain

LECTURES

2011 / 12 ***Lecturer in New Media,*** HfG Offenbach, Germany
Offenbach University of Art and Design,

2010 ***Workshops at NYCResistors,*** New York, USA

2009 ***Guest Lecture at Pratt Institute,*** New York, USA
Information Technology and Creative Practices (ITCP)

AWARDS AND PROJECTS

2011 ***Awarded 2nd Prize, Venice Design Week,*** Venice, Italy

2011 ***Recognition Award,*** ABoT, Artists' Books on Tour,
Österreichisches Museum für Angewandte Kunst (MAK), Vienna, Austria

2009 ***Art Territory,*** Art Residency Vilnius,
European Capital of Culture 2010, Lithuania

EXHIBITIONS (SELECTION)

2012 ***Capri Art Projects***, Projektraum Stilper, Frankfurt am Main, Germany
After the Sunset, COLLECTIVA gallery, Berlin, Germany
(entre nous), Literaturhaus Frankfurt am Main, Germany
ABoT, Artists Books on Tour, Museum of Decorative Arts in Prague (UPM), Czech Republic
Luminale, Heyne Kulturfabrik, Offenbach, Germany
ABoT, Artists Books on Tour, International Centre of Graphic Arts (MGLC), Lubljana, Slovenija

2011 ***ABoT***, Artists Books on Tour, Österreichsches Museum für angewandte Kunst (MAK), Vienna, Austria
Liquid/Segni, Venice Design Week, Venice, Italy
in light and in gloom, KorridorGalerie, ATELIERFRANKFURT e.V., Frankfurt am Main
Sigh, COLLECTIVA gallery, Berlin, Germany (solo)
Edith Kollath, Arte Santander, Santander, Spain
Ever tried. Ever sighed. DMY International Design Festival, Berlin, Germany
noting will ever be the same, Fresh Paint Contemporary Art Fair, Tel Aviv, Israel
Bedevilment In Paradise, Proteus Gowanus, New York, USA

2010 ***Try Again, Fail Again***, Kunstverein Hildesheim, Germany
come out – within, Schmiede Wettig, Nieder-Olm, Germany (solo)
Viennafair 2010, COLLECTIVA gallery, Vienna, Austria
the book as its own addendum, Marwen, Chicago, USA
Arduino – a lineage, NYC Resistors, New York, USA

2009 ***again, again***, COLLECTIVA gallery, Berlin, Germany (solo)
Ringen, Cream Contemporary, Berlin, Germany
things and thougts, COLLECTIVA gallery, Berlin, Germany
nothing will ever be the same, HFBK, Hambürg, Germany

2008 ***property and evidence***, DamStuhltrager Gallery, Brooklyn, New York, USA (solo)

2007 ***Smilefaucet – AIR***, Fontana's, New York, USA

2006 ***Frisch vom Tisch***, Kunstverein Hannover, Germany

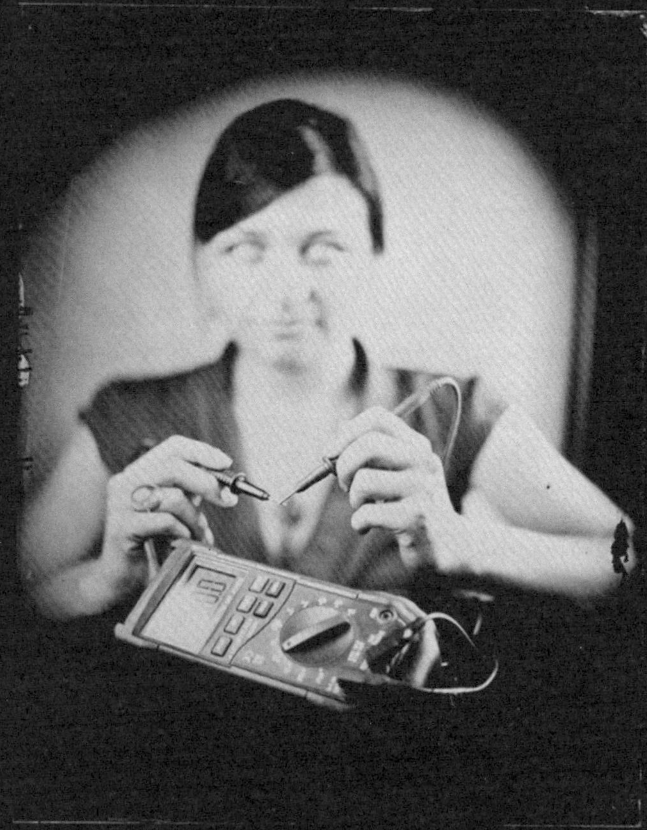

EDITH KOLLATH

Tin Typ/Ferrotypie by/von Melitte Buchmann, New York 2009

AGAIN, AGAIN

2009
truck awning,
programmed steam
engine,
dimensions variable

BW 1

2006
video loop
1'48"

DISPORT

2009
motors, textiles, wood,
aluminum, programming
320 × 430 × 430 cm

DUETT, BIBLE & KORAN

2006
video loop
1'24"

IF IT WERE A SHEET OF PAPER

2011
dark mirror, wooden
box, silk paper, magnet
30 × 40 × 30 cm

IN BETWEEN

2007
video loop
1'38"

LIGEIA

2010
piano wire, textile ribbon
100 × 20 × 20 cm

NOTHING WILL EVER BE THE SAME

2009
fabric, electronic
mechanism
height variable × 220 ×
220 cm

PENDULUM LUCIDUM

2011
iron frame, casted light
bulbs, programming
60 × 90 × 40 cm

SIGH

2011
paper, epoxy, fibreglass
dimensions variable

THINKING I'D LAST FOREVER

2008 – ongoing
antiquarian books,
electrical mechanism
approx. 10 × 20 × 30 cm

TRYING TO EXPAND THE POTENTIAL OF LOVE

2011
semitransparent mirrors,
wood, casted light bulb
80 × 25 × 20 cm

THE UBER-SEXY ENTRANCE EXPERIENCE

2013
aluminum, copper, iron,
brass, textiles, electronic
mechanism
dimensions variable

UNTITLED (TAPE-TEXT)

2010 – ongoing
collage on black paper
35 × 18 cm

UNTITLED (TAPE)

2010 – ongoing
collage on black paper
35 × 28 cm / 105 × 84 cm

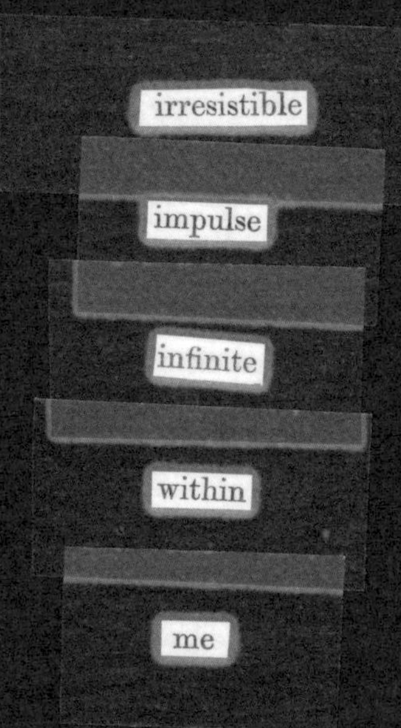
irresistible
impulse
infinite
within
me

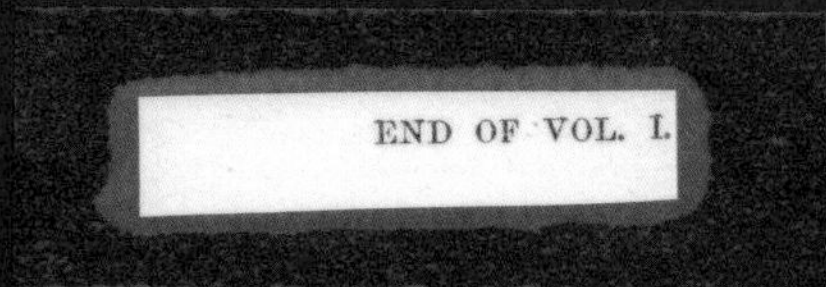

END OF VOL. I.

EDITOR / HERAUSGEBER

COLLECTIVA, Berlin

CONCEPT / KONZEPTION

Edith Kollath & COLLECTIVA, Berlin

GRAPHIC LAYOUT / GESTALTUNG

Melanie Kollath

ESSAY / TEXT

Christina Grammatikopoulou

TRANSLATION INTO GERMAN / ÜBERSETZUNG INS DEUTSCHE

Katja Bendels

COPY EDITING / LEKTORAT

Madhu Kaza (English)
Adrian Hoffmann (German)

PHOTO CREDITS / FOTONACHWEISE

Edith Kollath & COLLECTIVA, Berlin

IMAGE EDITING / LITHOGRAFIE

against interpretation

PRODUCTION / GESAMTHERSTELLUNG

Pinguin Druck, Berlin

GEDRUCKT AUF / PRINTED ON

Munken Lynx
by Arctic Paper
www.arcticpaper.com

KINDLY SUPPORTED BY / MIT FREUNDLICHER UNTERSTÜTZUNG DURCH

Hessisches Ministerium für Wissenschaft und Kunst

Stadt Frankfurt am Main – Dezernat für Kultur und Wissenschaft

DISTRIBUTION / VERTRIEB

Gestalten, Berlin
www.gestalten.com
sales@gestalten.com

PUBLISHED BY / ERSCHIENEN IM

DISTANZ Verlag
www.distanz.de

ISBN 978-3-95476-040-4
Printed in Germany

MY THANKS TO / MEIN DANK AN

Raphael Abrams, Felix Bösel, Ewa & Timo Bojarowski, Michael Brühl, Maren Esdar, Madhu Kaza, Hanne & Wolfgang Kollath, Melanie Kollath, Bre Pettis, Alexander Stefas, Maike Tiedemann, Ulrike Walther, Stefan Wlaschiha, Shira Zelwer und an viele weitere helfende Hände und Geister / and to all further helping hands and minds.

Ohne euch wäre – auf die ein oder andere Weise – nichts von alledem möglich geworden! Danke. In one way or another, none of this would have been possible without you! Thank you.